Interfaith Wedding Ceremonies:

Samples and Sources

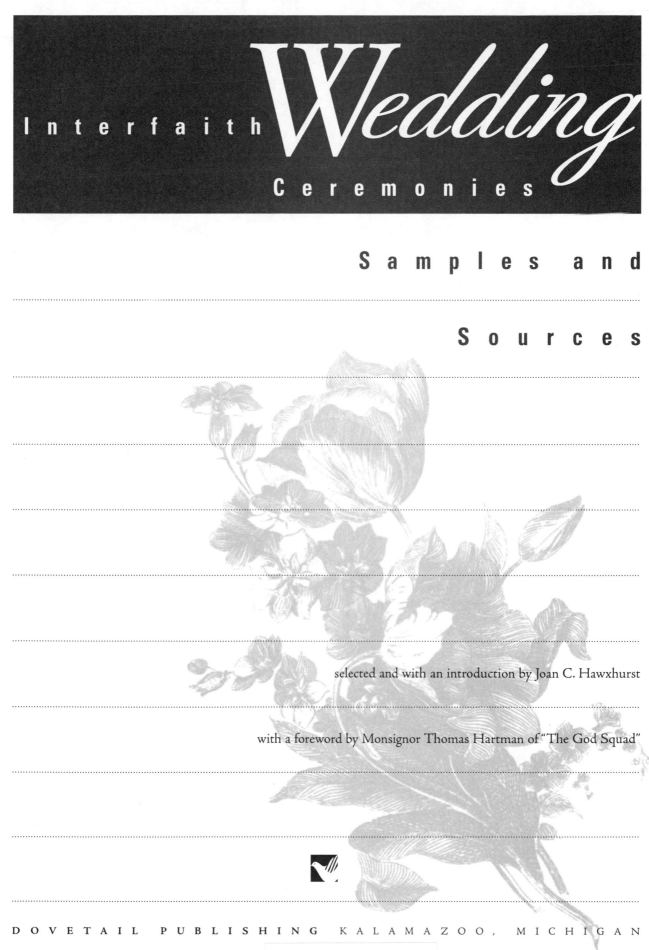

Interfaith Wedding Ceremonies

Samples and Sources

selected and with an introduction by Joan C. Hawxhurst

with a foreword by Monsignor Thomas Hartman of "The God Squad"

DOVETAIL PUBLISHING KALAMAZOO, MICHIGAN

DEDICATION

This book is dedicated to my husband, Steve Bertman, whose presence by my side on our spiritual journey makes the interfaith path-breaking worthwhile.

ACKNOWLEDGMENTS

This book was inspired by all the hopeful, deeply committed interfaith couples who have called and written to *Dovetail* over the years looking for resources and support as they planned their wedding ceremonies. Their courage, persistence and optimism in the face of resistance from their families and their faith traditions is truly heartening.

The compilation of ceremonies in this book would not have been possible without the generous help of many, many interfaith couples and of numerous Christian and Jewish clergypeople. I would especially like to acknowledge the hard work and the editorial guidance of Mary Heléne Rosenbaum, Noah Saunders, and Rabbi Allen Secher. For their work on behalf of interfaith couples, I am grateful to Rabbi Irwin Fishbein, Father John Cusick, Father Paul Colloton, Rabbi Charles Familant, Father John Hester, Rabbi Harold White, Reverend Bruce Epperly, Reverend Ken Fell, Rabbi Dr. Jonathan Romain, Reverend David Matthew, Rabbi Steve Mason, Father Albert Ruschman, and the countless other clergy who are committed to working with interfaith couples as they prepare to marry.

A special thanks to all the couples who so graciously shared their ceremonies and their stories with us: Kathy and Allen Feibelman, Karen McCarthy and Dan Kowal, Joanne McAndrews and Lawrence Eisenman, Susannah West and David Powell, Kathryn and Lance Flitter, Nancy Nutting and Harry Cohen, Helen and Tom Shibley, Pam and Larry Rosenberg, and the members of the Chicago Jewish-Christian Couples' Dialogue Group: Patty and David Kovacs, and Renita Gordon and Michael Miller, among many others.

It is rare and wonderful to work with a book designer who understands the delicacies of life in a "mixed" relationship, and I am thankful for the beautiful influence of Janie Bynum on this book.

Without the constant support and gentle humor of *Dovetail's* "right-hand" woman, Alison Siragusa, this book would still be a glimmer in the editor's eye.

And thanks, finally, to my two extended families, who have worked hard to understand and respect my own interfaith marriage.

Contents

CONTENTS (Continued)

FOREWORD

by Monsignor Thomas Hartman

Congratulations and Mazel tov on your upcoming wedding!

The journey on which you're about to embark will be both the most exhilarating and the most difficult of your life. You and your fiancé will be dedicating your lives to each other. You will be sharing your hearts, minds, and souls. You will be promising to help and encourage each other to love yourselves, others and God. It's an exciting—and demanding—time.

If you had come to me before you met your fiancé and had asked my advice, I'd have said marriage is tough enough—marry within your faith. But life doesn't always work out that way. You have fallen in love with someone of another faith. You want to get married. Okay. Then set about to do right by yourselves, your families, and your God.

Together you have to examine your family backgrounds. You have to ask yourselves why you want to be married to each other. You have to ask if this relationship helps you to grow, to love, to become a better person. Your interfaith marriage will be more challenging because you come from differrent cultures, traditions, and religions. How are you going to raise the children? Will your families accept your decisions? How will you practice your faith after you are married? Sadly, too many couples don't face these issues. Instead, they avoid discussions of religion and faith.

In a successful interfaith marriage, both partners are willing to talk with each other about their beliefs and their religions, even if the discussion is difficult or painful. In this context, an interfaith wedding can be a sign of hope, a reminder to all of us that, if we are willing to make the effort, the barriers which separate us can indeed be broken down. As a Christian and a Jew, you take on special challenges and opportunities. You face the challenge of living with two different, and sometimes contradictory, sets of beliefs. You have the opportunity to be an example to the world of successful interfaith dialogue at a very personal, day-to-day level.

When a couple comes to me to be married, I feel privileged to be a part of the preparation for marriage. I try to help couples understand that there are two levels of a wedding—fact and mystery. People who attend your wedding will know the fact of your love and the fact of your marriage. What you need to do is explore the mystery, the inexplicable connection and commitment that has been happening in your hearts and souls. If people don't know any more about the two of you after your wedding than they knew before, you and your wedding officiant will have failed. You will have created a ceremony, but not a loving, spiritual ritual.

As you plan your interfaith wedding ceremony together, and as you embark on a new life together, each of you can be a spiritual guide to the other. The answer to the challenges you will face is not to abandon your faith. It is to embrace your individual faiths and to teach each other. If you can't begin doing that during your courtship, don't get engaged. If you can't come to some common ground during your engagement, don't get married.

I believe that interfaith marriages can succeed, but not easily. You'll have to work hard. Pray hard. Love hard. Read this book. Speak with your clergy. Get involved in your wedding plans. And get involved for the rest of your lives in charity, in prayer, in renewing your love, and in making your marriage a sign that people from different faiths can love with uncommon devotion, understanding and faith.

Monsignor Thomas Hartman is a frequent guest on ABC-TV's *Good Morning America*, co-host of "The God Squad" on nationally syndicated cable television, and co-author of *Where Does God Live? Questions and Answers for Parents and Children* (Liguori, Missouri: Triumph Books, 1991) and *How Do You Spell God? Answers to the Big Questions From Around the World* (New York: Morrow Junior Books, 1995).

CHAPTER ONE

GETTING STARTED

ou've met a wonderful person and fallen in love. Your future looks bright and clear. Of course you realize you have religious differences, but with careful and loving discussion, you know that you can live with them. You'll build a home where both of your faiths are respected and understood. But when you proudly announce your engagement and begin to plan your wedding, the conflicts start to surface.

Your mother calls your wedding canopy a rose trellis, his mother calls it a huppah. You want a full Catholic mass, but then you remember that his family won't be allowed to take communion. He'd like to include a recitation of the traditional Jewish wedding blessings, but you're afraid your family will be put off by the Hebrew. Your local pastor has agreed to officiate at your wedding, but she has no experience with the Jewish traditions you'd like to include. If these scenarios sound familiar, then this book is for you.

This book is for interfaith couples concerned about the content of their wedding ceremonies, couples who want their families' two traditions to be respected and included in their own special and unique ceremony. Other books can help you with invitations, rings, and receptions. Other books can provide you with lists of readings and musical selections (we offer a list of some of the best sources in our extensive appendix). This book can help with the words and the symbols that convey what you believe as you start your interfaith marriage together. And it can help you create a wedding ceremony that is a wonderful, meaningful ritual for you, your extended families, and your guests.

CREATING A MEANINGFUL RITUAL

[Editor's note: I am grateful to Noah Saunders for his input into this section.]

Rituals nourish and enrich our lives. When we purposefully and mindfully ritualize our behavior, even the simple can become sacred. Rituals are a way of getting in touch with what is important to us.

Joseph Campbell writes: "People say that what we're all seeking is the meaning of life. I don't think that's what we're really seeking. I think that what we're seeking is an experience of being alive, so that our life experiences on the purely physical plane will resonate within our innermost being and reality, so that we actually feel the rapture of being alive."

Rituals are the recurring events—the actual passages of our lives, such as birth, school graduations, marriage, retirement, and death—that bring to light many of the essential questions of our life: Who am I, what am I doing here? What is right and wrong, and how do I know? How do I give meaning to my life? These questions arise from within us. In contemplating them, we connect with our inner being and get closer to feeling the rapture of being alive.

The asking and answering process we go through when we participate in the wedding ritual sanctifies our existence within the universe. By being conscious of how many generations have experienced a similar gathering of family and friends for our ancestors' weddings, we can mindfully and even religiously experience the deep connection we have with others—now, before us, and after us.

By mindfully engaging in our own wedding ritual, we enter a mythic reality in which truth is much more than factual. If the ceremony is genuine and meaningful, all involved can feel the exhilaration of new life and new possibilities. We connect with those around us in a profound way because we are experiencing the same deep sense of being alive, prompted by the marriage ritual in which we are involved.

When they look upon a man and woman getting married in a meaningful and personal ceremony, guests come to understand their role as witnesses and participants in a life cycle and a social transition that has prevailed for centuries in keeping our families and communities diverse and growing. This connectedness—with ourselves and with others—can guide us as we embrace and reconcile the differences and the similarities among our religious beliefs. We can bring a "living spirit" to our celebrations, and by mindfully crafting our interfaith ceremony, we can transform it into a ritual.

At some point in the wedding ceremony, it is useful to remind the couple, within earshot of their guests, that their months of plans and efforts are resulting in a profound change, not only in their own lives but in the lives of everyone else in attendance as well. This is not meant to be a grandiose statement. Instead, it is an affirmation of our ability as individuals to influence and direct our own lives, and, to a lesser extent, other people's lives. In the context of the wedding ritual, such a realization by couples—that they can have an effect on their lives—takes on a mysterious and mythic reality unreachable in everyday experience.

In this decade of exploding openness, as more and more people reach across religious and cultural barriers to choose a mate, wedding ceremonies are changing too. Couples are looking to include more spiritual meaning in their wedding rituals. A January 1996 survey conducted by *Modern Bride* magazine found that 85 percent of all engaged couples choose to have a religious ceremony, as opposed to a civil ceremony. Very few couples, interfaith or not, simply take what their chosen officiant offers them in terms of a ceremony—couples want to be involved in making their wedding ceremony something that is personally meaningful to them.

In response to this trend, many officiants and wedding consultants have developed their own "notebooks" of selected readings, vows, and homilies, and they offer these valuable resources to couples who come to them for help in designing their wedding ceremonies. This book draws on a number of such resources. It also draws extensively on actual ceremonies researched and written by interfaith couples who have chosen to be actively involved in the design and execution of their wedding services.

MAKING THE MOST OF YOUR ENGAGEMENT

No matter how many resources or sample ceremonies you review while creating your own wedding service, you can gain a lot from this exciting process. As you and your fiancé become involved in designing your own wedding service, you can spend a great deal of time and energy learning, not only about the beliefs and traditions with which each of you were raised, but also about each other's values, dreams, and goals.

> *The winter before our May wedding, my fiancé took a new job in Colorado. We left the East Coast and drove across the country, with our prized possessions on the back seat of our Honda. That "car time" was precious to us, and we spent a big chunk of it dreaming about our wedding day. We kept a pad and pen with us, and as we drove, we wrote out lists of who we'd invite, what readings and music we'd include, and how we'd arrange the seating for our families. Most importantly, we thought together about what we believed, why we were getting married, how we were creating one home that respected and included our two faiths, and how we could share all this with friends and family through our wedding ceremony. We laughed, we fought, and we cried. It was a difficult and wonderful trip, and by the time we reached Colorado, we had fashioned the basis of a meaningful and inclusive ceremony.*
>
> *—partner in an interfaith marriage*

Not everyone has the luxury of a long car trip, with no ringing telephone or work deadlines, to plan their wedding ceremony. But you certainly can carve out some time to think together about the meanings of the ritual you are about to share. For interfaith couples, this time is crucial, for each of you brings a different and deeply-felt set of traditions and beliefs that must somehow be brought together, in a wedding ceremony and in a shared life.

So set aside some time for each of you to explore this book. As you go through the different ceremonies, you'll find ideas, passages, and explanations that you like, and others that don't seem to fit for you. Talk with your partner about the things that are meaningful to you. Use your reactions to the different ceremonies included here as stepping-off points to discuss your feelings and your beliefs. As you begin to create your own wonderful ceremony, you will also learn valuable lessons about each other, lessons that will last long after the rings are exchanged and the rice is thrown.

These lessons are important, and you should take advantage of those who can help you as you learn them. If the person you ask to officiate at your wedding offers premarital counseling, take her or him up on it. If your officiant doesn't offer such counseling, find someone— a professional counselor or therapist—who will spend several sessions with you and your fiancé, probing the difficult issues you'll face as an interfaith family. You'll want to talk openly with your partner about everything from money matters (you may be surprised at how differently two cultures look at this question!) to how you'll raise your children. If you can't find a local source for premarital counseling on your own, call the American Association of Pastoral Counselors at (703) 385-6967 for a referral in your area.

We cannot stress enough how important this premarital exploration is to a successful interfaith marriage. As you begin to share with your fiancé, you may find you have a hard time expressing the details of your religious background. You're not alone. Most of us are never pressed to talk about what our faith means and why. Most of us hesitate to discuss our own beliefs for fear of damaging the precious relationship we are nurturing. But if you don't talk about what you believe now, it will come back to haunt you in the years to come. So, if you find that you can't tell him why you feel you have to have a priest bless your rings, or if she just can't understand why the chuppah is so important to your vision of your wedding day, seek out resources that can help both of you understand your respective religions. Some useful books are listed in our appendix.

One point that will be quite helpful for your and your fiancé to remember is that, unlike most North American Christians, Jewish Americans make a distinction between being culturally Jewish and being religiously Jewish. Of course, those who are religiously Jewish are also culturally Jewish. But many modern Jews consider themselves culturally, but not religiously, Jewish—that is, they don't attend synagogue regularly, they don't keep kosher, and so on. However, one never hears a Christian making a distinction between being culturally and religiously Christian!

For both Christians and Jews, there is yet another layer of consideration—one's ethnic background. On the east and west coasts of the United States, for instance, distinctions are made between the Roman Catholic Church and the Irish Catholic Church. Similarly, Jewish people's ancestors came from such diverse countries as Russia, Poland, and Spain. Each of these cultures has its own identity and its own way of living its religious beliefs. You and your fiancé each need to understand your own and learn about your partner's cultural, ethnic, and religious identities.

When people warn you about the perils of intermarriage, we urge you neither to close your eyes and ears nor to run scared, but instead to think as carefully as you can about whether any of these perils apply in your case.

— Judy Petsonk and Jim Remsen,
The Intermarriage Handbook

As you begin this learning process, do not avoid the tough questions. Instead, show your partner how much you love and trust him or her by opening up about these deeply personal issues. You might choose to use the following list of questions to help you get started:

+ What are your goals in life?

+ What are the values you hold most important?

+ What aspects of your partner's character do you most cherish, and why?

+ What is important to you about your religion?

+ Describe your image of God.

+ Do you and your family agree on your religious beliefs?

+ What do you know about your partner's religion? Are there elements of his/her religious beliefs that you disagree with or find unacceptable?

- What do you see as the cultural differences between the two of you? (specifics might include money, tastes, family and in-laws, child-rearing, food, sexuality, among others)

- How do you envision the family that you and your partner will create?

- What does your extended family mean to you? How do you feel when you visit your partner's family?

- Have you talked about children? How will you raise them? What religious training, if any, will you give them?

- What are some of the issues on which you've already discovered disagreement? How will you negotiate these? Are there any which cannot be resolved?

- What made you decide to marry?

- What does marriage mean to you?

- What does it mean to be someone's life partner?

You can also learn from the experiences of others. Well before your wedding day, seek out other couples who have been happily intermarried for at least several years. You may wish to contact an interfaith support group in your area (start with the list of groups in our appendix). Of course, interfaith couples can help you with the details of your wedding, but don't stop there. Talk to interfaith couples who have children. Ask them about how they've dealt with their religious and cultural differences. Ask them about the difficult decisions they've made about home life and children's education. The advice and insight such experienced interfaith couples can provide will help you and your partner grow together long after your wedding day.

In an interfaith wedding, even the details can be laden with meaning. The huppah under which this couple stands was created out of a quilt hand-sewn by the bride's grandmother out of scraps of fabric from five generations of women in her family.

"THINK AGAIN" CHECKLIST

You should seriously think again about marrying out of your faith if:

1. You secretly hope maybe someday s/he'll convert.

2. You feel an affectionate (or not) contempt for anyone who could really believe that guff (otherwise known as your partner's religion).

3. You tell yourself, "S/he's not as bad as most of them."

4. You figure that how you raise your kids will work itself out, and besides, maybe you won't have any.

5. You think what your parents think doesn't matter.

6. You think what society thinks doesn't matter.

7. You think religion doesn't matter to you—and never will.

8. Talk about religion makes you nervous, bored, embarrassed, or angry.

Reprinted with permission from *Celebrating Our Differences: Living Two Faiths in One Marriage*, by Mary Heléne Rosenbaum and Stanley Ned Rosenbaum, Boston, KY: Ragged Edge Press and Black Bear Productions, 1994.

CHAPTER TWO

CHOOSING AN OFFICIANT FOR YOUR WEDDING CEREMONY: WHAT YOU CAN EXPECT

hen you and your partner decide to get married, one of the first hurdles you'll face as an interfaith couple—and potentially one of the hardest to surmount—is the choice of an officiant for your wedding ceremony. Especially if the Jewish partner feels strongly about having a rabbi take part in the wedding ceremony, you should prepare yourselves for an emotional search. But first, since whom you choose to officiate will reflect your desires for the content of your ceremony, you'll first need to spend some time sketching out each of your visions for your wedding day.

Here are some questions to get you started:

- What do you want to communicate about your relationship through your wedding ceremony?

- Do you want a formal or informal ceremony? Religious or secular? If religious, what does that mean to each of you: a specific denomination's ceremonial structure? non-denominational? spiritual, but without mention of God?

- How important is it to have a representative from each of your religious traditions present at your ceremony? participating in some way in your ceremony? leading your ceremony? Why is this important?

- What traditions, if any, from each of your religions and cultures do you want to include? How does the Christian partner feel about there being Hebrew in the ceremony? How does the Jewish partner feel about the name of Jesus being mentioned in the ceremony?

- How will each of your families participate?

Once you have answered these questions, you'll be able to make a better decision about the type of ceremony with which you both feel comfortable. Following are the basic choices for your wedding ceremony. Most interfaith couples choose one of the first two options.

1. CHOOSE ONE RELIGIOUS TRADITION.

If only one partner feels strongly about his or her religious identity, you can choose to have a wedding in only that tradition—either a Jewish wedding or a Christian wedding. In this case, you will need to find a representative of only one of your faith traditions. By choosing to have either a Jewish or a Christian ceremony, you will bypass many of the

> A Christian ceremony, whether Catholic or Protestant, has at its core the sacrament of marriage, similar to other basic church sacramental rituals in that it is rooted in the Christian belief in Jesus as savior and in the salvation this belief will bring. . . . The Jewish wedding focuses not on the religious beliefs of the couple but rather on their future as a political entity, so to speak, within the Jewish community. Because the ceremony signifies the creation of a new Jewish family unit, the wedding is seen strictly as a Jewish occasion; according to Jewish law (halakhah), it is the joining of two Jews. If one partner is not Jewish, the union is invalid; the religious laws joining the couple are binding only on Jews.
>
> — Susan Weidman Schneider, *Intermarriage: The Challenge of Living with Differences between Christians and Jews*

objections raised by clergy about interfaith weddings, so it should be easier to find an officiant. And sometimes, an officiant in this position will graciously agree to include elements from the other partner's tradition. A Catholic priest or Protestant minister will probably be willing to let you break a glass at the end of the ceremony or stand beneath a wedding canopy. And sometimes a rabbi or cantor will allow a reading or a song from the Christian tradition (although no mention of Jesus would be appropriate). You'll find some examples of this type of inclusion in the sample ceremonies in Chapter Four.

Be aware, however, that the partner who chooses not to include his or her own religious tradition in the wedding ceremony may later regret or resent this decision. If you decide to go this route, make sure that you think through, as individuals and as a couple, what this decision means for your life together after your wedding day. Are you deciding that you will celebrate only one religion as a family? Are you deciding about possible conversion of the partner whose faith is not represented in the ceremony? How will each of you feel if the uncommitted partner experiences a renewed interest in his or her religious tradition after you are married?

If you choose not to include your own traditions in the ceremony, do not keep that decision from your parents. Fill them in on the content of your ceremony in advance, so that they are not stunned on the day of the wedding.

2. BALANCE BOTH RELIGIOUS TRADITIONS.

If you are both committed to your individual religious traditions, you can choose to have a representative from each of your faith traditions at your wedding ceremony. This is one of the most difficult, and yet most popular, choices made by interfaith couples.

In most parts of the country, it is not easy to find a rabbi willing to co-officiate with a Christian minister in such a ceremony. In some large metropolitan areas, however, Christian and Jewish clergy who have teamed up in support of interfaith families actually end up developing strong relationships with each other and with the community of intermarried families in their area. In metro areas like Washington DC, Chicago, and San Francisco, Christian/Jewish clergy teams are available to help interfaith couples with their weddings, as well as with religious rituals later in life, like baby namings and coming-of-age ceremonies.

If you are able to find a Jewish and a Christian officiant willing to work together, you will almost always discover that the search was well worth the effort. Intermarried couples who spend the time and energy to create a ceremony that incorporates what is important to each partner from their respective religious traditions usually feel that their ceremony is the most

> The benefits which come from a ceremony which brings together successfully the resources of two faiths will far outweigh the problems which may be associated with planning such an event. Altogether too many couples sacrifice a significant chance to grow in the name of "making it easier" for both families. To compromise one's spiritual foundations or to abandon them completely may result in a ceremony which is unsatisfying to one person or the other and healing for neither. We urge you to do your best, working with the people who will officiate at your interfaith wedding, to be sure the ceremony does everything possible to offer an affirmation of the best of both ancient traditions.
>
> — David Glusker and Peter Misner, *Words for Your Wedding*

memorable part of their wedding day. And most clergy who consent to co-officiating at an interfaith ceremony are very helpful when it comes to selecting readings, scripture and rituals that come together in a meaningful, inspirational ceremony.

3. HAVE TWO CEREMONIES.

If you are both committed to your individual religious traditions but cannot find clergy willing to co-officiate, you can schedule two separate ceremonies. Only one will be legally binding, so the second ceremony is technically a "blessing" of the marriage. A rabbi who is not willing to officiate at your full-blown, legally binding wedding ceremony may be willing to bless your marriage afterwards in a smaller ceremony, perhaps at the site of the reception. Or a small civil ceremony with a Jewish flavor might be followed by a religious Catholic (or Protestant) ceremony. These alternatives may be a diplomatic way to maintain the separation between your two religious heritages while helping both partners—and both families—feel respected and included.

4. FIND A "NEUTRAL" RELIGIOUS TRADITION.

Some interfaith couples choose to be married in the Unitarian Universalist Church, or the Ethical Culture Society, because these traditions are inclusive and embracing of both Jewish and Christian beliefs. A couple can have a traditional, yet neutral, "non-denominational" ceremony.

5. HAVE A CIVIL CEREMONY.

If your religious traditions are not central to your vision of your wedding day, you can avoid some religious difficulties by having a civil service with a judge or a justice of the peace. Some civil officiants are even willing to include simple religious traditions or readings in their standard ceremony. Be aware that you may lose the "pomp and circumstance" of a religious wedding.

6. CONDUCT YOUR OWN WEDDING CEREMONY.

You can have a private legal service, in a judge's chambers or at a mayor's office, with only yourselves and perhaps close friends or family as witnesses. Once the legal aspect of your marriage is complete, you can have free rein over a larger public ceremony of your own design and leadership. You can combine whatever elements of your two traditions you desire, and choose whomever you want to preside over the ceremony. In fact, in some states it is now possible to marry yourselves lawfully without a legally sanctioned officiant—you can officiate at your own wedding! When you are inviting guests to a ceremony that is neither religiously nor legally binding, it may be seen as courteous for you to tactfully inform them of this (so that they don't feel "cheated out of the real thing").

> When people of differing backgrounds come together, it is because something of great value is shared. Expressing what the two of you hold common and what in you is different but compatible can make for an outstanding ceremony.
>
> — Sydney Barbara Metrick,
>   *I Do: A Guide to Creating Your Own Unique Wedding Ceremony*

What to Expect When You Ask a Minister

Since it is such an important event in your lives, you, if you are like most engaged couples, probably want to have some religious representation at your wedding. Riding on the wave of newfound love and commitment, most interfaith couples are caught unprepared for the response they receive when they approach their local clergy about being a part of their ceremony. If you have not yet asked anyone to officiate at your wedding, be forewarned. You are about to learn, if you aren't already aware, that your engagement elicits very different responses from different clergy representatives.

From the Christian community, by and large, you'll receive a supportive response. Ministers and priests in all but the most conservative denominations have come to accept the reality of interfaith marriage. And since the percentage of Christians who marry outside the Christian faith is miniscule, Christian clergypeople do not feel that their faith tradition is threatened by your decision to reach beyond the fold. A minister or priest may ask you some tough questions, and may insist on thorough premarital counseling ("pre-Cana," it's called in the Catholic church), but he or she will almost certainly consent to being part of your wedding ceremony.

That's not to say that you won't have to do a little prodding. For Catholics, this may mean helping clear Church obstacles, like paperwork and dispensations, out of the way. Catholics who wish their interfaith wedding to be binding in the eyes of their church must request a special dispensation. Father Peter Meehan, a Catholic priest in Manhattan and co-author of *Happily Intermarried: Authoritative Advice for a Joyous Jewish-Christian Marriage*, suggests you visit your local parish priest armed with knowledge. "Your official parish, where you have the right to be married, is where you live now—even if you haven't been going there regularly. All official things have to be channelled through it. Your parish is not where you were born, the city where you are to be married, or where your mother lives, or at the university where your cousin the priest works. It is where you live."

"All priests in the world can assist at an interfaith marriage, if they're official," continues Father Meehan. "If necessary, they can do the paperwork to make themselves official. And if all the proper papers are filed, a priest does not even have to be present for a wedding to be officially recognized by the Catholic Church. (This was not the practice 25 years ago.) So when you go to the rectory door, instead of looking for a priest to marry you, look instead for someone who will help your wedding to be officially recognized and who will be able to assist in making preparations that reflect your spiritual values."

Some Protestant denominations have made great efforts to educate their clergypeople about interfaith marriage and to provide a welcoming atmosphere for intermarrying couples. The Presbyterian Church (U.S.A.) has even produced a special resource for its members and ministers, which proclaims that, "in the contemporary world, characterized by global interdependence and the daily interaction of people of differing cultures and religions, interfaith marriage may create networks of families never otherwise so related. It is not possible to dismiss events across the world when circumstances affect the family or larger community of a daughter's or son's spouse. In this sense, intermarriage may tighten the web of the human family and the care, concern, and knowledge of people—God's people—in the global village. Interfaith marriage can provide an opportunity for growth and change."

WHAT TO EXPECT WHEN YOU ASK A RABBI

Expect a very different response if you decide to approach a rabbi about participating in your wedding. Even if you ask your family's long-time rabbi, he or she may well refuse your request. While it may be difficult to see past the hurt this causes, try not to take your rabbi's decision personally. It is part of a much bigger—and very complex—issue. The majority of the Jewish community, as you probably have already sensed, sees interfaith marriage as a danger to be avoided. Orthodox and Conservative rabbis almost never officiate at interfaith weddings. While most Reform and some Conservative rabbis embrace interfaith couples *after* they are married, few will consent to being part of the wedding itself.

In 1995 the Rabbinic Center for Research and Counseling in Westfield, New Jersey, sent a detailed questionnaire to 1,794 Reform and Reconstructionist rabbis across the country. Of this number, 334 rabbis, or 47 percent of the rabbis who responded, said that they officiated at intermarriages under certain specified conditions. Thirty-nine percent do not officiate but are willing to refer to rabbis who do, and 14 percent neither officiate nor refer. Data collected in this survey suggest "that the number of rabbis who refer to other rabbis is increasing and that significantly fewer rabbis require, as a condition of officiating, that children be raised as Jews or that the rabbi be the only officiant."

One important point for you and your partner to clarify before looking for a rabbi is this: do you both want a Jewish and a Christian officiant at your wedding, or would you be satisfied with a rabbi as the sole officiant? This question is important for you to answer, because only a few rabbis will co-officiate with a Christian clergyperson. More rabbis will officiate on their own at a "Jewish-style" interfaith wedding—where there is a wedding canopy and Hebrew blessings, but the marriage contract is a civil one rather than a ketubah—but often only if you promise to raise your children as Jews.

Interfaith marriage is the most hotly debated issue for American Judaism today, and it is worthwhile to learn why, especially if you'd really like to have Jewish representation at your wedding. Following are the very different opinions of three rabbis on the topic of intermarriage.

> Interfaith couples should realize that their presence generates some strong and ambivalent feelings among even the most liberal rabbis and synagogue leaders. Couples need to accept that synagogues are not guilty of religious bigotry when they insist that certain rituals can be performed only by Jews. Memories of an unpleasant experience in one synagogue should not diminish an interfaith family's search for a communal setting in which to live out the Jewish part of their heritage.
>
> — Rabbi Harold Kushner, author of *Who Needs God*

"I REFUSE TO OFFICIATE AT INTERFAITH MARRIAGES."

Rabbi Barry Baron, Houston, Texas

My welcome, and my congregation's, is the same for interfaith couples as for all others: come and join us in belonging, growing, learning and believing in a God who stands for us, cares about us, calls us to a covenantal relationship, and asks us to work for the perfection of creation. Notwithstanding this welcome, I do refuse to officiate at interfaith marriages, and I am grateful for the opportunity to explain my reason.

In Jewish tradition, the marriage ceremony is known as "Kiddushin." The word has two meanings, "betrothal" and "sanctification." In Judaism, marriage is a holy act, or mitzvah, desirable to God and governed by Jewish law. Jewish law was conceived by my rabbinic forebears as encompassing the behavioral norms which God desires of Jews.

Rabbinic authority to officiate at marriages derives from rabbinic responsibility to administer Jewish law. The title "rabbi" implies the bearer's allegiance to that law. Jewish law sanctions the marriage of Jews to each other, and, as a rabbi, I feel that I can only officiate at marriages which Jewish law sanctions.

Then why do I welcome interfaith couples who seek to join my synagogue? The answer is that I am seeking to respond to the environment in which I find myself. My world is not the world of my ancestors. I live in an open society in which all kinds of people meet, date, live with and marry one another. In the United States, individuals of many races, religions, and ethnicities are marrying each other in record numbers. Boundaries between groups are more permeable than ever before. My Judaism, and my Jewish community, need to respond creatively to this reality, not only so that they can survive, but also so that modern Jews with contemporary sensibilities can find meaning in their tradition and can use its teachings to make a difference in their world.

My love for Judaism stops me from officiating at interfaith marriages even as it leads me to reach out and embrace interfaith couples. There are many other rabbis in the United States who substantially share my views on these issues. Our stance does not please everyone. Many people have told me that I cannot expect interfaith couples to feel welcome after marriage if I send them away at the point of marriage. I cannot answer this assertion directly. I can only say that the force of tradition which leads me that way is the same force for deeper spirituality and meaning in my life and the lives of others, including many who are in interfaith marriages.

"I OFFICIATE WHEN COUPLES STATE THEIR INTENTION TO RAISE CHILDREN AS JEWS."

Rabbi Emily Korzenik, Stamford, Connecticut

Jewish intermarriage is currently estimated at 52 percent, and Jews are now only 2 percent of the national population, with a very low birthrate. These figures are much discussed, studied, and lamented, but all too little is being done to address the matter constructively. We can respond wisely, warmly, and effectively to intermarriage and the children born of those marriages.

The Jews survived miraculously as a people because we have been capable at once of distinctiveness and assimilation. Lately, however, in general the leaders of the Jewish community have been exclusive when we should be inclusive. Too often we have been rejecting, although rejection is always bruising and almost always futile. Indeed, rabbis do not claim that their refusal to participate in wedding ceremonies is preventive. They are acting from conviction and/or according to the rules. The rabbinic guidelines for all denominations state that rabbis should not officiate at intermarriages. The Reform and Reconstructionist rabbinic organizations do not discipline those who digress. In any case, the majority of rabbis feel that participation at the weddings of interfaith couples would suggest approval and be contrary to their understanding that Jewish ceremonies are to be performed only for Jews.

But rabbis must be receptive from the beginning. We cannot turn people away, then "grudgingly" accept the couple after the fact, and expect that there will be no scars, no residue of resentment. Granting that our attitudes are born of millennia of persecution and fear for our survival, these rejecting attitudes are neither gracious nor productive. In his most recent study of intermarriage, sociologist Egon Mayer presents statistics indicating that it makes no difference whether or not rabbis officiate at interfaith weddings. It is not simply that more rabbis should perform wedding ceremonies. The rabbis must give time and effort to create bonds and establish expectations.

Since intermarriage most often takes place between a Jew and a nominal, uncommitted Christian, these marriages should be regarded as opportunities. Indeed, it is not uncommon that the non-Jew becomes the catalyst whereby the Jewish partner begins to define, study, and vitalize his or her Jewish heritage.

One thing is sure: when a caring Jew and an uncommitted nominal Christian marry, there is a real likelihood that a sturdy Jewish family will emerge. Why should we not make every effort to encourage and assure that eventuality?

The Jewish community, its leaders and institutions must respond affirmatively. As a rabbi, I have chosen to spend time and energy counseling interfaith couples. When such couples state their intention to raise any future children as Jews, I am willing to officiate at their wedding ceremony.

"I OFFICIATE IF COUPLES AGREE TO PREMARITAL COUNSELING."

Rabbi Charles Familant, San Francisco, California

Rabbis who perform intermarriages in this country are still very much in the minority, and they have no standard requirements. Some rabbis require attendance of classes in Judaism prior to the wedding. Others want assurances that the children will be raised as Jews. Still others require premarital counseling.

Premarital counseling is my sole requirement, whether or not both parties are Jewish. My chief concern is that, as responsible adults, a couple is capable of resolving issues in a manner which enhances the marriage. At some point in this process, I deal with the questions which inevitably arise: How is it that I came to perform intermarriage ceremonies when other rabbis say they cannot?

Some contend that opposition to intermarriage is one of the mainstays against assimilation. However, when people turn to me for assistance, they have almost always already made a decision. To decline their request does not prevent their marriage but, in the case of the Jewish partners, denies them the opportunity to reconnect with their Jewish roots, often after years of estrangement. In the case of the non-Jewish partners, opposition to intermarriage leaves the impression that rabbis and Judaism are discriminatory and devoid of compassion, thus destroying any incentive for further learning.

Jews marrying non-Jews often become more keenly aware of their Jewish identity than might have been the case if they had married Jews. They request books on Judaism and attend workshops on Jewish practice. It is not a foregone conclusion that intermarriage necessarily leads to the loss of Jewish identity, either of the Jewish partner or of the offspring.

Discussions on intermarriage tend to overlook the fact that the partners have an enormous amount in common. Some, after years of dating people from their own religious and cultural backgrounds, have discovered in their chosen mate a far deeper bond, in comparison with which cultural and religious similarities seem quite minor.

As a species, we are becoming increasingly aware of our common bonds and interdependence, which transcend national, cultural, and religious concerns. Recognition of this fact is a necessary condition for our human survival. Intermarriage, as an aspect of this larger phenomenon, should therefore not be construed as an unavoidable evil but as a potential good, even if it does not contribute to the survival of Judaism as we know it today. The integration of different religious traditions may result in the emergence of new forms of religious expression. Whatever becomes of Judaism in the future, those aspects that have enduring value may well leave their indelible stamp on any newly emerging forms.

Moreover, if Jews—especially Jewish leadership—adopt an attitude toward this growing trend which recognizes the legitimacy, rights and motivations of intermarrying couples, then many from this vast and growing population may find a place within the Jewish community. It will require a revamping of our institutions and a greatly changed Judaism. Judaism has changed often throughout its long history in response to the shifting currents in the world. That has been both its challenge and its key to survival. Once again it has the opportunity to meet such a challenge.

(The above opinions are excerpted from the February/March 1993 issue of *Dovetail: A Newsletter by and for Jewish/Christian Families.*)

If, after reading these rabbis' opinions, you feel very committed to having a Jewish presence at your wedding ceremony, ask yourselves why. Do you feel the need to demonstrate your ongoing commitment to Judaism to the Jewish side of the family? Do you feel the need to "balance" a Jewish influence against the Christian elements of the ceremony you are planning? Do you feel drawn to Jewish wedding traditions, like standing under a huppah and breaking a glass? Some of these reasons can be satisfied without a rabbi as co-officiant at your ceremony. Perhaps you could ask your local rabbi, not for his presence at your ceremony, but for help with writing the Jewish portions. You can probably include traditional Jewish elements, like the huppah and the glass, without a rabbinical presence—just ask your officiant. And it's possible that, even after a rabbi has turned down your request to co-officiate, she or he will attend your wedding to demonstrate support for you, thus providing an unofficial Jewish presence.

> **Simply put, the American Jewish community perceives intermarriage as a threat and is frightened. The fact that predictions about the imminent demise of the Jewish people date from ancient times does not allay these fears, in part because the openness of American society poses an unprecedented challenge to the maintenance of a distinct Jewish identity.**
>
> **— Anita Diamant,**
> ***The New Jewish Wedding***

If you still feel that you'd like to have a rabbi co-officiate at your wedding, it probably can be done. Ask around—chances are that other interfaith couples in your area have already done a search for sympathetic local rabbis. If you can't find interfaith couples on your own, read through the society pages of your local newspaper, noting the weddings performed by both a rabbi and a minister or the names of couples who are obviously interfaith (like McCarthy and Goldberg). If you can track them down, call these newlyweds for more information on their officiants.

In most states, some cantors are legally able to perform marriages, and you may find one willing to help you. But cantors are usually governed by the same institutional restrictions on intermarriage as rabbis.

Be forewarned: a few rabbis who co-officiate at interfaith weddings, especially those who advertise, can demand large fees for their services while providing little guidance and support before or after your wedding day. You may be faced with the choice of paying a lot of money for someone who is not very helpful to you, or not having a rabbi at your wedding. If you are contacting a rabbi you've found in an advertisement, ask in a tactful way if you may speak with other couples he or she has married, and then find out from these couples how much help they received.

You may find an out-of-town rabbi willing to come to you, but again, be prepared to pay hefty fees and all travel-related expenses. (Just for the sake of comparison, according to *Modern Bride* magazine, the average cost of a formal wedding in 1995 was $17,634, of which $273 went to fees for clergy, church, or synagogue.)

Of course, most rabbis are not going to officiate at your wedding for the money. There are rabbis who legitimately want to reach out to interfaith couples, usually because they see this as a way to show couples that they are welcome in the Jewish community.

MAKE YOUR BEST CHOICE

Your wedding is a celebration, and when approached mindfully and with the intent to engage the participation of everyone present, your wedding ceremony can become a meaningful ritual. Your participation in writing your own wedding and in getting to know the officiants (and they, you) will bring warmth, genuineness, and connectedness to all present.

But remember, your wedding is a celebration and ritual, not a performance. Your officiants should not see your wedding ceremony as an opportunity to impose their arbitrary preferences and songs. Choose your officiants carefully, making sure that they're committed to focusing on the two of you and your guests as the prime reasons and focus for your celebration.

By the day of your wedding, if not sooner, you should be secure and relaxed in the knowledge of what your wedding ritual and celebration will entail—the events and significances of each stage of the ceremony; your officiants' ability to comfortably and joyously lead you, your »wedding party, and your guests with clarity and purpose. You should feel that all details are being taken care of by your officiants, allowing the two of you to focus on being connected to one another in your heart and your spirit.

Couples have widely differing experiences with the officiants they choose.

> *A Protestant woman from Oklahoma married her Jewish fiancé in her grandmother's home. Looking back, she wishes that she had incorporated more religious traditions, both Christian and Jewish, into the ceremony. "It was cold, even though the justice of the peace was good." The couple had been unable to find a rabbi willing to officiate at their ceremony, and although their minister was willing to participate, the couple decided that having only Christian clergy representation was not fair to the Jewish family. If she had it to do over, she would "find someone to represent both sides and make it more meaningful."*

A Catholic woman from northern Virginia remembers her disappointment that the priest who co-officiated at her wedding ceremony was not more supportive. The rabbi, she wrote, was the best part of the ceremony—"everyone loved him," but the priest was there "under duress." He was 30 minutes late for the ceremony, and she was afraid he wouldn't show. If she had it to do over, she would "seek out a sympathetic priest while we were still dating."

You and your partner will have to decide on which of the options listed in this chapter makes the most sense for you. While you are in the middle of this decision, you may feel hopeless about getting what you want, and one or both of you may end up compromising your original ideas about who would lead your ceremony. But remember that once you've chosen the officiant for your wedding, you'll be able to move on to the exciting task of planning your ceremony. And no matter who officiates, you can still create a meaningful, inspiring service that communicates your goals and dreams as an interfaith couple.

Notes

....

....

....

....

....

....

....

....

....

....

....

....

CHAPTER THREE

DESIGNING YOUR INTERFAITH WEDDING CEREMONY: WORKING WITH TWO TRADITIONS

nce you have decided on the type of ceremony you want and have chosen the officiant, you will work closely with this person or persons to design the order of events for your special day. Your officiants will probably provide you with sample ceremonies and lists of readings, scriptures, and musical selections from which to choose. If they are not already familiar with it, you should share with them this book, so that they are aware of the variety of wedding ceremonies that have been created by other interfaith couples and their officiants.

Following is a combined list of events that might occur in an interfaith wedding service. It includes events from Protestant, Catholic, and Jewish wedding ceremonies. This list is intended only as a starting point to help you begin to think about the order of your ceremony. You may wish to skip some of the events listed, rearrange certain events, and/or add other ideas of your own.

ORDER OF WEDDING CEREMONY EVENTS

Processional

Welcome/Opening Statement

Address to the Couple

Opening Prayer/Invocation

First Candle Lighting

Reading(s)

Expressions of Intention by Bride and Groom

Recognition of Family and Guests

Homily/Remarks

Marriage Vows

Reading and Signing of the Ketubah

Blessing and Exchange of Rings

Lighting of the Unity Candle

Pronouncement of Marriage

Prayer/Blessing for the Marriage

Sharing of Wine

Benediction

Presentation of the Couple

Breaking of the Glass

Kiss

Recessional

Intimacy

The key, say many couples who've been through [creation of an interfaith wedding ceremony], is to establish an atmosphere that's reverent but not superreligious.

— Jennifer Rogers,
   Tried and Trousseau:
   The Bride Guide.

A Note on the Jewish Wedding Liturgy

While nearly all of the established western Christian religions have an extensive and pre-established wedding ceremony liturgy, this is not true of contemporary Jewish wedding ceremonies. According to Talmudic law, the requirements for a Jewish couple to be married in the eyes of the Jewish community are only three. First, the groom gives the bride something tangible, such as a ring, which (when the law was established) had to be worth at least 200 shekels. The groom then speaks the ancient prayer to his bride—"By this ring, as a token and pledge of my constant love, you are consecrated to me as my wedded wife, according to the laws of Moses and Israel." Lastly, these first two acts must be witnessed by at least two people who are not related to each other or to the bride or groom. According to Jewish law, a Jewish couple is considered to be marrying themselves. Unlike most Christian wedding ceremonies, no one, not even a rabbi, is required to officiate at a Jewish wedding.

Except for the exchange of the wedding rings and the blessing that accompanies the ring exchange, there is no established liturgy for Jewish weddings. As a result, every synagogue wedding you attend will have different language, different components, and different rituals. In modern times, these Jewish wedding rituals usually include a welcome blessing, a blessing over the wine, the reading of the seven wedding blessings, the exchange of the rings and the speaking of the ancient prayer mentioned above, the signing and reading of the ketubah or marriage contract, and a benediction. Other aspects of modern Jewish weddings include conducting the ceremony under a huppah and breaking a glass at the conclusion. While an exchange of vows is not required or expected in a Jewish wedding, many modern Jewish weddings include marriage vows.

It is important to keep in mind that the rituals and wedding components of today's Jewish and Christian weddings are for the most part modern constructs. The Christian church was not formally involved in the wedding ritual until the 15th century. Prior to that time, weddings were civil rather than religious or church-related.

There are many connections between the ancient Jewish laws of marriage and the rituals that evolved over time in the Christian community. As a brief example, a canopy, essentially identical to the huppah, was used in all French Catholic Church weddings during the 15th century. So as you create your interfaith wedding ceremony, remember that modern religious wedding ritual is just that—modern, and not steeped in ancient history. Furthermore, the roots of many common wedding traditions are unclear, and many of the explanations we use for modern wedding rituals have been developed long after the rituals first came into use. For example, see the many explanations given for the Jewish custom of breaking a glass at the conclusion of the wedding ceremony, as listed in Chapter Six.

LOCATION OF YOUR CEREMONY

One early decision you'll need to make is where to have your ceremony. You may find that you, your officiant, or your family are not comfortable with conducting your wedding in a church or synagogue. Often a church sanctuary has a prominent cross, which will probably make the Jewish family uncomfortable. Sometimes the cross can be removed or covered with a banner, rendering the sanctuary more "neutral." Some couples have shunned the sanctuary in favor of a church reception hall for their ceremony. Other options for the location of your ceremony include: college chapels (nondenominational), clubs (like country clubs), museums, catering halls, parks, boathouses, mountaintops, waterfalls, scenic overlooks, private homes, private gardens, academic facilities, and hotel ballrooms.

Your choice of location can affect the order of events in your ceremony. For example, if you choose to marry outdoors, you'll probably want to skip any candle-lighting—a gentle breeze could blow out your newly lit unity candle! If you are being married in a synagogue, you should know that the more traditional a Jewish congregation is, the less likely the synagogue is to have an organ or piano for musical accompaniment, though you should be able to bring in instrumentalists and vocalists yourselves.

> **When we began to plan our wedding, all of a sudden it seemed that we weren't going to be able to please both sides. She was not going to convert to Judaism, and I was not converting to Catholicism. So first of all, with her not being Jewish, I couldn't find a rabbi who would marry us, not even a Reform rabbi. And since she felt that the only way she would be married in the eyes of her church was to have the wedding in a Catholic church, I gave in on that.**
>
> **— partner in an interfaith marriage**

REFLECTIONS FROM OTHER INTERFAITH COUPLES

Who better to ask about planning an interfaith wedding ceremony than couples who have already done it? When readers of *Dovetail*, an independent national newsletter devoted to issues of concern to interfaith families, were asked to share their reflections on their wedding days, several common threads emerged. Almost everyone who responded to *Dovetail*'s questions was pleased with the—sometimes unexpected—positive responses of their families on their wedding day, even when families had been distant or disapproving beforehand. Couples who created their own "blended" ceremonies were almost universally pleased with the results, and often cited their interfaith ceremonies as the "best part" of their wedding day. On the other hand, couples whose ceremonies included more traditions and/or representation from a single faith were wistful about the lack of balance. Below we will examine the intricacies of each of these aspects of planning an interfaith wedding ceremony.

Involving Parents

Many interfaith couples find that working with their two families is one of the greatest challenges they face in designing their wedding. Perhaps you are among the interfaith couples for whom one or more of your family members responds negatively to your engagement announcement. Take heart from the fact that while it is fairly common for a family member to threaten to boycott the wedding, he or she almost always comes around before the day of the ceremony. Gently but firmly remind this family member that your wedding will occur with or without his or her presence.

Rabbi Steven Carr Reuben, author of *Making Interfaith Marriage Work*, who has been counseling interfaith couples for twenty years, says he has never known of a case "in which the decision of parents not to attend their child's wedding changed their child's mind or prevented the marriage from taking place." Perhaps you can tactfully convey this fact to your recalcitrant family member. Ask him or her to put aside disagreement for this one day—your wedding day. In this way you'll all promote the healing and family bonding that is possible through the wedding ritual.

Being Sensitive to Two Traditions

Talk with your families early on in the process of designing your ceremony, and listen to their views and expectations for your wedding day. When you and your partner have decided the best way to proceed, lovingly discuss your decisions and the considerations behind them with your families, so that they can understand your choices. By being open and honest with both families from the beginning, you will minimize inquisitive probings by family members, as well as wedding day surprises.

You can help your two families become comfortable with your wedding plans by respecting their traditions and by asking for their input. For example, as you work out the wording of the blessings and prayers you include in your ceremony, you may well want to avoid Trinitarian language or direct reference to Jesus by name, as this will usually make your Jewish family and guests uncomfortable. Most Christian clergy are comfortable using only references such as "Lord" and "God," which are appropriate in both religions. If there are parts of the ceremony about which you have no strong preferences, invite your families to help make decisions about these parts.

To help both families feel comfortable, many couples work hard to create a wedding program that includes explanations and transliterations, so that

A major difference between the two traditions is the style of the processional. If you adopt the Jewish custom of having both parents of both bride and groom come down the aisle with them, and stand under the canopy together if there is one, guests may be intrigued by the symbolism of the joining of the two families, rather than the feudal holdover of "giving" the bride from one man to another. Our own daughter and son-in-law opted for the Orthodox practice of having the two mothers walk with the bride, and the two fathers with the groom, rather than each set of parents with their own child, to emphasize this coming-together-of-families theme for our largely Christian clan.

An older couple, particularly if this is not a first marriage, might want to consider an early Christian practice recently revived: the bride and groom begin the service seated separately, with their respective families, in the congregation, and are "called out" by the officiant.

— Adapted with permission from *Celebrating Our Differences: Living Two Faiths in One Marriage*, by Mary Heléne Rosenbaum and Stanley Ned Rosenbaum.

guests at their ceremony can understand and participate in traditions with which they are not familiar. Some ideas for your program are included in Chapter Six.

You can make sure that you schedule your ceremony at an appropriate time. Most Jewish families consider having a ceremony during the Sabbath, which runs from sundown Friday to sundown Saturday, to be inappropriate. Some Christian families may object to a Sunday service. Many interfaith couples opt for a Saturday evening ceremony and reception.

Also, the date you choose for the wedding may be affected by the liturgical season. Some Christians disallow marriage during Advent or Lent. Many Jews exclude the ten days between Rosh Hashana and Yom Kippur and the fifty days (excluding Lag b'Omer) between Passover and Shavuot.

Your menu at the reception should be sensitive to dietary restrictions. If the Jewish family keeps kosher, don't serve pork or shellfish, and keep meat and dairy foods separate. If the Christian family doesn't drink alcohol, don't serve it, or set up the bar in an unobtrusive location. If either family disapproves of mixed dancing, consider a chamber music group or a romantic strolling soloist.

Says Noah Saunders, who officiates at hundreds of interfaith weddings each year in Colorado, "We can choose to honor our parents, grandparents, and other ancestors by acknowledging our roots and preserving the order of traditions, or we can choose to forget them, as many Americans have, in the interest of individualistic self-expression. It's our call."

He continues, "Your wedding presents the ideal opportunity to rediscover your roots and to revive some of the symbols and rituals that have special meaning for you, your families, and your community."

Sometimes you may find it difficult to gauge your parents' and in-laws' feelings about your impending marriage. If they appear hesitant or distant, they may actually be waiting for you to draw them into the planning process. One intermarried woman, when asked about what she would do differently if she had her wedding to do over, reflected on her civil ceremony performed by a Jewish judge, and said that she would have "involved more people, like our parents, in the ceremony. At the time, they did not appear to wish to be involved."

Sometimes, on the other hand, your parents' or in-laws' wishes are all too clear. When asked about the worst part of her wedding, another intermarried woman wrote that "the ceremony was much too Jewish, with too many Hebrew words. Many people there thought I had converted!" If she had it to do over, this woman would "keep my mother-in-law completely out of the plans. I allowed her to plan the ceremony, and she gave us basically a Jewish wedding."

An intermarried man remembered that "my mother wanted to know why we couldn't be married in a social hall or other neutral ground. Her mother was disappointed that we weren't going to have a full mass. It seemed that everybody around us was having problems with the way we were going to do the ceremony. Finally we realized that, when it came down to it, the wedding had to do with the two of us. That knowledge helped us through the rough spots." Your wedding *does* have to do primarily with the two of you. And if you can remember this *and* include your families, so much the better.

ON WRITING THE CEREMONY

One woman who has been intermarried for 18 years remembers that the best part of her wedding day was "the ceremony, which we had written ourselves." Aside from the anxiety about whether everything would go according to plan, she recalls "a perfect day." The ceremony was officiated by a New Jersey rabbi, and the families, who had initially expressed concerns about the difficulties of raising interfaith children, were present and supportive on the day of the wedding.

The best part of another couple's wedding was "our interfaith ceremony. We spent a lot of time working on the details because this was very important to both of us. We were thrilled with the result." They had expected their families "to be polite and respect our interfaith ceremony. We were surprised and delighted to see everyone from both families having such a good time and really enjoying each other's traditions."

A third couple remembers the best part of its wedding as "having both faiths strongly represented in one blended ceremony." This couple worked hard at "building our own special service," which included a minister from the bride's family's church and a rabbi from the groom's childhood synagogue. The bride has since converted to Judaism, and she wishes she had chosen "a more neutral location, not in the church like we did."

Perhaps the most important lesson that engaged couples can take from these experiences is that great care should be taken in the planning of the wedding ceremony itself. Rather than allowing extended family to guide the process, you as a couple should take it upon yourselves to work out between the two of you what you want to say with your ceremony. You should carefully choose officiants. You should work together to select readings and rituals that are meaningful to both of you. If you work together to discuss your values and identify what is meaningful to each of you in the wedding ritual, you will do much more than plan your wedding day. You will have a head start on the challenges and opportunities that will face you throughout your spiritual life together.

On the following pages, you will find many examples of what other interfaith couples have done. There are sample wedding ceremonies printed here in their entirety (see Chapter Four), as well as selected excerpts from a number of other ceremonies (see Chapter Five). You will probably find that you are drawn to certain styles. Perhaps you are more comfortable with traditional language ("I take thee to be my lawfully wedded wife"), or maybe you want contemporary wording ("I choose you to be my partner and my friend"). Perhaps you want a short, simple service, or maybe you want to include and explain all of the religious traditions from each of your backgrounds.

You'll find lots of alternatives here. We encourage you to mark or highlight the sections, passages, or ideas to which you feel drawn. Throughout the next sections, we've included places for you to scribble notes as you read. We wish you all the collective joy and satisfaction felt by the couples who have produced the works on the following pages. Happy planning!

Notes

....

....

....

....

....

....

....

....

....

....

....

....

CHAPTER FOUR

Sample Wedding Ceremonies

n the following pages you will find very different examples of what an interfaith wedding ceremony can be. Some choose to follow tradition closely; others stray farther from convention. Some include as many traditions from each religion as possible; others choose a simple, unadorned style. Some address God using traditional masculine pronouns, while others use a more egalitarian approach. Whenever possible, we have retained the original language and style of each ceremony, so that you can appreciate the diversity of approaches and options.

You may well find that you feel drawn to certain portions of different ceremonies, and you should feel free to create your own ceremony out of bits and pieces you find here. After you have read through the sample and selections here and marked what you like, you'll want to discuss all of this with your officiant. Together you'll be able to design a ceremony that fits your personal style and conveys the important messages you want to send at the beginning of your married life.

A note about the Hebrew: Because most interfaith couples leave the reading of Hebrew at their wedding ceremony to a Jewish officiant or learned friend or family member, we have not included Hebrew texts or transliterations in the following ceremonies. Instead, we offer transliterations of a few of the most basic Jewish prayers in a special section of Chapter Five. If you choose to include Hebrew in your ceremony, you will want to discuss the details with your officiant.

[In interfaith marriages] both bride and bridegroom will let widen their mental horizons to make space for the new axis of their joined lives. Then the very process of putting together the ceremony can become a ritual of initiation into a life of examined, shared values. Readings and other personal contributions by the couple to one another can be like flags planted at the outermost boundaries of their hopes for the future.

— Eleanor Munro, *Wedding Readings*

The Wedding of Nancy and Harry / May 24, 1981
Officiated by a Priest

This ceremony was held in a Victorian mansion. The couple wanted the wedding held outside the church building in consideration of the Jewish relatives but also wanted a particular priest to officiate. They petitioned for and were granted a "dispensation of form" from the Catholic Church, which allowed them to depart from the usual way of doing things while still having a marriage recognized as valid by the Church. The ceremony contains no Hebrew, but does include Jewish elements, among them readings from Hebrew scriptures, songs from *Fiddler on the Roof*, and the breaking of the glass at the end of the ceremony.

Instrumental Prelude

Greeting

Priest: On behalf of the bride and groom, I'd like to welcome you here tonight.

In addition to witnessing marriage vows and celebrating with the couple, every wedding is a call to reflect on the First Lover, God. The processional song being used tonight was probably meant to be a love song between humans. But it describes a love so total, so faithful, so everlasting that it could only be on the part of the Perfect Lover. "Longer than there've been fishes in the ocean. . . I've been in love with you." Couldn't it be that God is singing this love song to us? As the wedding party processes in, we invite you to reflect on the many ways that God has shown His love for you personally.

Please remain seated.

Processional

"Longer" / Dan Fogelberg

[Bride and groom process in, each escorted by their parents.]

Candle Lighting

"Sunrise, Sunset" / J. Bock and S. Harnick

[Each set of parents lights a candle symbolizing their family tradition. During the last chorus, the bride and groom hug and kiss their parents and then move away from them to stand as a couple before the priest.]

Opening Prayer

Priest

Reading I

Genesis 2:18-24

(Theme: It is not good that man should be alone. . . . This is why a man leaves his father and mother and joins himself to his wife, and they become one body.)

RESPONSE

(Based on Jeremiah 29:11 and 31:3, Isaiah 54:10, Micah 6:8, and I John 4:12.)

Reader: I have loved you with an everlasting love. I have called you and you are Mine.

Congregation: I have loved you with an everlasting love. I have called you and you are Mine.

Reader: It is God who speaks:

> The mountains may depart,
>
> the hills may be shaken,
>
> but my love for you will never leave you
>
> and my covenant of peace with you will never be destroyed.

Congregation: I have loved you with an everlasting love. I have called you and you are Mine.

Reader: I know the plans

I have in mind for you,

plans for peace, not disaster,

reserving a future full of hope for you.

Congregation: I have loved you with an everlasting love. I have called you and you are Mine.

Reader: What is good has been explained to you.

This is what God asks of you—only this:

> to act justly
>
> to love tenderly
>
> to walk humbly with your God.

Congregation: I have loved you with an everlasting love. I have called you and you are Mine.

READING II

Colossians 3:12-17

(Theme: Be clothed in sincere compassion, in kindness and humility, gentleness and patience. Forgive each other. Over all these clothes, put on love.)

HOMILY

Priest (In his remarks, the priest talked about differences and our attitude toward them. If we view them as obstacles, they will divide and separate us. If we view them as complements, they will invite us to grow and become more whole and complete.)

STATEMENT OF INTENTIONS

Reflections from the bride:

What made our ceremony beautiful and meaningful was that we shared a lot of the meaning in the booklet we passed out to guests and in the actions we incorporated into the ceremony. For example, in the booklet we explained the symbolism in the design of our wedding rings, which we had commissioned from a designer who told us that "if you work as hard on your marriage as you have on these rings, you'll be in fine shape." At the start of the ceremony, people were touched when they heard the lyrics of "Sunrise, Sunset" as Harry and I physically moved from our parents' sides to a place of our own together.

EXCHANGE OF VOWS

Groom,
then Bride: Nancy/Harry, I love you.

And I look forward to being your friend and companion, your wife/husband and lover for life.

I promise to love you and respect you; to stand by you and be faithful to you; to be open and honest with you; and to always work toward our mutual growth.

I promise this with the help of God, for the good times and the bad times, till death do us part.

EXCHANGE OF RINGS

Priest: The history of the wedding ring is an interesting one. In prehistoric times, people tied a rope of grass around their waists, wrists, or ankles. Later this grass rope was placed on the finger. Still later the grass was replaced with flint, ivory, or amber.

In ancient Rome, the wife wore gold in public but iron at home, since it was more suitable for housework. In the early Greek Church, men wore iron as symbolic of strength and women wore gold, a weaker but more pure composition. Today, the custom of exchanging rings continues, with the circle symbolizing devotion and happiness unending.

LIGHTING OF THE UNITY CANDLE

"Sabbath Prayer" / J. Bock and S. Harnick

[The bride and groom take the flames from their parents' candles and light their own candle together.]

FROM OUR FRIENDS

[Representing the community and as a pledge of support, the couples who brought Nancy and Harry together—the "matchmakers"—offer some reflections.]

THE COUPLE'S PRAYER

Bride and
Groom: Lord, we stand before You today happy and hopeful, yet also somewhat scared. We believe that You brought us together and we know that You're with us now. We also know that the road ahead will have both good times and hard times. We ask now that You bless us and be with us in the following ways.

Help us to live up to the vows that we have made to each other today. Keep our love fresh, alive, and growing. Remind us always to approach each other with gentleness and patience. Teach us how to communicate and trust more completely. Never let us take one another for granted.

Guide us as we strive to hear You speaking to us through our religious traditions. Make us faithful to Yourself, as well as to each other. May our life together be a sign to others that people can live together in peace in spite of differences.

Make our home a place of peace and growth where people are always welcome. Help us reach out to others to share the love and blessings we ourselves have experienced.

If You bless us with children, make us good and loving parents. Help us always to remember that they are, first of all, Your children. Guide us as we try to raise them to be full and complete human beings aware of Your love. And help us to step aside when it is time to let go.

Thank You for our family and friends, both those present and those unable to be with us today. Their love and friendship has led us to be what we are today. May our celebration strengthen their awareness of Your love and their own commitment to love others.

And, finally, guide those present home safely at day's end. Amen.

Song of Blessing

"Forever Young" / Bob Dylan

Priest: "May you always do for others and let others do for you. . . know the truth and see the light surrounding you. . . have a strong foundation when the winds of changes shift. . . stay forever young." These and many more wishes are our prayer, not only for the bride and groom, but for their family and friends as well.

Final Blessing

Priest   [People respond with "Amen."]

The Wine Glass

(See page 69 for additional explanations of this tradition.)

Priest: Drinking from the wine glass and then crushing it is a Jewish tradition with many meanings. One is that it is a reminder of the hardships endured, particularly the destruction of the Temple in Jerusalem. Another can be summed up in "what has been will never be the same, can never be put back together." Finally, it serves as a reminder about marriage. Drinking the wine represents the joys and sweetness of life, and crushing the glass represents the hardships.

[Bride and groom each drink from the wine glass. Groom breaks the glass.]

Introduction of the Newlyweds

Recessional

Jig / Traditional

THE WEDDING OF HELEN AND TOM / JUNE 27, 1993
OFFICIATED BY A MINISTER

This ceremony took place outdoors under a huppah in an Oregon river valley. The couple arranged for choirs from two churches to come and sing.

PROCESSIONAL

Choirs: "Joyful, Joyful, We Adore Thee" / Beethoven

OPENING STATEMENT

Minister: We are gathered here today in the presence of God to give thanks for the gift of marriage, and to witness the joining together of Helen and Tom. In the Jewish and Christian traditions, marriage is a sign of our Creator's intention for wholeness in all creation. Out of the chaos, God brought order. That creative purpose is still at work. The joining together of two persons into one unique, intimate, and creative unity in marriage is therefore not only a symbol but also a demonstration of the well-being, the shalom, the purpose of human society. And so marriage is truly a celebration of God's good work in creation.

The uniting in marriage of two individuals from two separate families and backgrounds to establish a new family is an important and memorable event. For us, attached as we are to Helen and to Tom by special bonds of love and affection, the uniting of these two people in heart and body and mind is an occasion of great significance which we can all celebrate.

Marriage is not a casual event, nor is it simply a private affair between two individuals. Marriage is to be entered into responsibly and prayerfully. This marriage brings together this day two individuals, two families, and two communities of faith. It is, then, in the midst of a troubled and broken society, a sign of hope. It deserves and needs the support of a wider community. Today is a time for family and friends to share in their commitment to each other by offering Tom and Helen our continued support, love and best wishes in their lives together.

In their love together, which they publicly express in this ceremony, Tom and Helen demonstrate not only their joy in the present but their commitment to share the future together. We share their joy, and promise to do all we can to help bring to fulfillment a future of peace and justice for them and for all humanity.

PRAYER

Minister: Let us pray: O Lord our God, source of all blessing, in happiness and joy we thank you for the gift of marriage, which we celebrate today. May you give Tom and Helen the ability to rejoice always in their love. May you fulfill every worthy wish of their hearts. May you open their eyes to the beauty and the mystery of the love they hold for each other, every day as today. And may their life together embrace and nurture the promise of this moment, so that all who know them will call them truly blessed. Amen.

MUSICAL INTERLUDE

"Sunrise, Sunset" / J. Bock and S. Harnick

VOWS

Minister:	Helen, Tom, please state your intent to enter into this union by expressing your vows to one another. Helen, repeat after me: "I promise, Tom, before family and friends, to commit my love to you; to respect your individuality; to be with you through life's changes; and to nurture and strengthen the love between us, as long as we both shall live."
	[Helen repeats vow.]
	Tom, repeat after me: "I promise, Helen, before family and friends, to commit my love to you; to respect your individuality; to be with you through life's changes; and to nurture and strengthen the love between us, as long as we both shall live."
	[Tom repeats vow.]

Witnesses' Vow

Minister:	(To the congregation) Will all of you witnessing these vows do everything in your power to uphold Tom and Helen in their marriage? Will you?
Congregation:	We will.

RINGS

Minister:	The wedding ring is a symbol of unity, a circle unbroken, without beginning or end. And today Tom and Helen give and receive these rings as demonstrations of their vows to make their life one, to work at all times to create a life that is whole and unbroken, and to love each other without end.
	Tom, take this ring and place it on Helen's finger, and state your pledge to her, repeating after me: "This ring I give you as a sign of our constant faith and abiding love."
	[Tom repeats pledge.]
	Helen, take this ring and place it on Tom's finger, and state your pledge to him, repeating after me: "This ring I give you as a sign of our constant faith and abiding love."
	[Helen repeats pledge.]

PRAYER

Minister:	Eternal God, without your grace no promise is sure. Strengthen Tom and Helen with patience, kindness, gentleness, and all the other gifts you so abundantly impart, that they may fulfill the vows they have made this day. Keep them faithful to each other and to you. Fill them with such love and joy that they may build a home of peace and welcome. And guide them by your word to serve you all their days. Amen.

PRONOUNCEMENT OF MARRIAGE

Minister: Before God and in your presence as witnesses, Tom and Helen have made their solemn vows to each other. They have confirmed their promises by the joining of hands and the giving and receiving of rings. Therefore I proclaim that Tom and Helen are now husband and wife.

[Best man moves glass.]

BENEDICTION

Minister: [Minister makes a brief mention of meaning of breaking of the glass—see page 69 for some ideas.]

And now may the Lord bless you and keep you. May the Lord make his face to shine upon you and be gracious unto you. May the Lord lift up his countenance upon you and give you peace this day and all your days. Amen.

BREAKING OF THE GLASS

[Tom breaks the glass.]

Minister: You may kiss!

RECESSIONAL

Notes

....

....

....

....

....

....

....

....

The Wedding of Jean and Robert / October 18, 1992
Officiated by a Judge

Note that this ceremony, despite the fact that it is a civil one without religious representation, includes a candle-lighting ritual and the breaking of a glass.

Welcome and Address to Couple

Judge: Dear friends, we are gathered here today to celebrate the drawing together of two lives. We have come so that this man, Robert, and this woman, Jean, may be united in marriage. This commitment is not to be entered into lightly, but with certainty, mutual respect, a sense of reverence, and perpetuality.

Robert and Jean, as you know, no minister, no priest, no rabbi, no public official can marry you. Only you can marry yourselves. By a mutual commitment to love each other, to work towards creating an atmosphere of care, consideration, and respect, by a willingness to face the tensions and anxieties that underlie human life, you can make your wedded life come alive.

Your love for one another and your willingness to accept each other's strong points and weaknesses with understanding and respect will help cement the foundation for a strong and lasting marriage. Learn to respect your individual outlooks. Share your thoughts, experiences and dreams with one another. Cherish the intimacy and understanding that comes with the passage of time. As you enter this union your belief that marriage is a partnership between equal individuals with common goals, hopes, and dreams will give your lives special meaning and fulfillment.

Today, there is a vast unknown future stretching out before you. That future, with its hopes and disappointments, its joys and its sorrows, is hidden from your eyes. But it is a great tribute to your faith in each other that you are willing to face these uncertainties together. May the love with which you join hearts and hands today never fail, but grow deeper and surer with every year you spend together.

Candle Lighting

Judge: A marriage brings together two individuals, with separate lives, to perform the lifelong pledge of uniting as one. These candles before us symbolize the union of your marriage. The two outer candles represent the two of you, Robert and Jean, as individuals. The center candle, which you will kindle together, represents the unity which will continue to develop as you are married. The external candles will remain lit, to show that, even in your unity, you may also remain as individuals.

[Robert and Jean light candle while music is played.]

Reading

I Corinthians 13

EXCHANGE OF VOWS

Judge: Will you join hands, Robert and Jean, and repeat after me:

I, Robert, love and cherish you, Jean,

For being all that you are,

All that you are not,

And all that you can be.

Know that I am here for you,

And that your pain will be mine,

And your joy mine as well.

All I ask is you—your love—your trust—your caring.

I choose you to be my wife

Till death do us part.

[Robert repeats vow.]

I, Jean, love and cherish you, Robert,

For being all that you are,

All that you are not,

And all that you can be.

Know that I am here for you,

And that your pain will be mine,

And your joy mine as well.

All I ask is you—your love—your trust—your caring.

I choose you to be my husband

Till death do us part.

[Jean repeats vow.]

EXCHANGE OF RINGS

Judge: The perfect circle of a ring symbolizes eternity. Gold is the symbol of all that is holy and pure. As you give these rings to each other, our wish is that your love will be as eternal and everlasting as these precious rings. In the years to come, they will remind you of the overwhelming joy of this special occasion. May you always be as happy together as you are today.

Robert, please repeat after me:

This ring symbolizes our union—for today, tomorrow, and all the years to come. You are now my life partner, my beloved, my friend. With this ring, I thee wed.

[Robert repeats pledge.]

Jean, please repeat after me:

This ring symbolizes our union—for today, tomorrow, and all the years to come. You are now my life partner, my beloved, my friend. With this ring, I thee wed.

[Jean repeats pledge.]

BREAKING OF THE GLASS

Judge: Stepping on this glass signifies remembering the past and moving to the future. You no longer belong to your parents' houses, but to your own.

[Robert smashes the glass.]

DECLARATION OF MARRIAGE

Judge: Robert and Jean, having witnessed your vows of love and faith to each other, by the power vested in me, it is my joy and personal privilege to pronounce you husband and wife. You may now kiss the bride.

Notes

....

....

....

....

....

....

....

....

....

....

....

The Wedding of Pam and Larry / October 8, 1994
Officiated by a Minister and Rabbi

Processional

Welcome

Rabbi: [Rabbi speaks in Hebrew and in English. See page 70, no. 1, for transliteration of the Hebrew.]

Blessed are you who come in the spirit of love.

Let us rejoice and feel the sanctity of this moment.

From the very depths of our being, we pray that Pam and Larry will prosper in their life together as husband and wife.

Minister: In this sacred hour, and at this special moment in time, we open our hearts to Pam and Larry. They have come here with special gifts: their love, hopes, and dreams and their faith in one another. May they be moved to give and share, to grow together as a couple and as individuals. May they share their experiences, their enthusiasm, and their feelings openly with one another and thereby find life's deepest meaning and richest happiness. May the covenant which Pam and Larry now seal be blessed with trust and devotion. And may their lives be bound together in love and understanding. Amen.

Rabbi: On behalf of Pam and Larry, I welcome you all here today. Pam and Larry symbolize a lesson in love and harmony, encouraging all of us to seek a common bond. They come before us with a spirit of human unity, a respect for the tradition of marriage, a strong love for each other, family and friends, and a faith in God common to each of their respective educations and upbringings. Every marriage ceremony is a unique event. But today, not only are two unique individuals joined together, but two faiths as well.

Minister: Pam and Larry, by the very fact of asking both a minister and rabbi to witness your exchange of vows, you are asking us to join you in expressing to your families and friends that each of you considers your religious traditions to be precious. In marriage you are not sacrificing your commitment to these traditions, but rather reaffirming them and promising to share what is real and vital, the best of both traditions, with one another.

Rabbi: I also wish to say to the family and friends of Pam and Larry that this is your service as well as theirs. The future of their home together depends also upon you. No marriage can thrive alone. Through your thoughts, your feelings, and your acts, you can strengthen their bond. Pam and Larry welcome your wisdom and strength to help their love grow, for it is through this love that they themselves have grown.

[Rabbi explains the meaning of the huppah, mentioning that Pam's father and Larry built it together.]

READINGS

I Corinthians 13

Ruth 1:15–18

(Theme: "Your people shall be my people, and your God my God.")

VOWS

Rabbi: [Explains that Pam and Larry have also signed a ketubah or marriage contract, and that this ketubah was written especially to express the feelings of interfaith couples. Reads the following pledge they have made by signing the ketubah.]

We pledge to each other to be loving friends and partners in marriage; to talk and listen, to trust and appreciate one another; to respect and cherish each other's uniqueness; and to support, comfort and strengthen each other through life's sorrows and joys. We further promise to share hopes, thoughts, and dreams as we build our lives together. May we grow our lives ever intertwined, our love bringing us closer. We shall endeavor to establish a home that is compassionate to all wherein the flow of the seasons and the passages of life, as witnessed by our mutual traditions, are revered and honored. May our home be forever filled with peace, happiness and love.

(Text reprinted with permission from the *Interfaith Ketubah*, Good Company, Chicago, Illinois)

Pam and Larry, have you come before us today, freely and without reservation, to give yourselves to each other in marriage?

Pam and Larry: We have.

Minister: Please join hands and face each other.

Larry, do you take Pam to be your wife, your best friend and your love? Will you commit your life to her, embracing all the joys and sorrows, all the triumphs and hardships; and will you love, honor, and be faithful to her for the rest of your life?

Larry: I do.

Rabbi: Pam, do you take Larry to be your husband, your best friend and your love? Will you commit your life to him, embracing all the joys and sorrows, all the triumphs and hardships; and will you love, honor, and be faithful to him for the rest of your life?

Pam: I do.

Reflections from the Bride:

We were married in a beautiful outdoor ceremony at a state park, surrounded by friends, family, curious campers and even a few deer! We had a Protestant minister and a rabbi—we were lucky that a local hospital had a Jewish chaplain who would do the ceremony. Both officiants gave us ideas for creating our own ceremony, and the following is what we came up with. The transcription of the Hebrew pronounciation came from the rabbi, and it really helped the minister follow along. It was a beautiful, memorable ceremony, made even more special by the fact that there was a part of each of our faiths included.

BLESSING AND EXCHANGE OF RINGS

Minister: These rings are in the shape of a circle, symbolizing a love never ending.

Rabbi: These rings are also made of gold, suggesting a quality about them that is priceless. It is our hope that your love will be of such quality that it will inspire a life together without measure.

Minister: Larry, repeat after me. This ring symbolizes the unending union of my life with yours. Your dreams are now my dreams. Your hopes are my hopes. And your love is my blessing.

[Larry repeats pledge.]

Rabbi: Pam, repeat after me. This ring symbolizes the unending union of my life with yours. Your dreams are now my dreams. Your hopes are my hopes. And your love is my blessing.

[Pam repeats pledge.]

Minister: May these rings which you have exchanged be a constant reminder of the blessing of friendship you have found in each other, and serve to assure you that in a changing world, your love, like the circle on your fingers, is constant.

Rabbi: Because you have pledged yourselves to a life of concern and caring, it is my pleasure to pronounce the traditional Jewish blessings of marriage.

[Rabbi pronounces the seven wedding blessings in Hebrew. See pages 66-68 for various translations. Minister pronounces blessings in English.]

Pam and Larry share the ceremonial cup of wine, as their family and officiants look on.
Photo by David S. Thomas.

KIDDUSH (SHARING OF WINE)

Rabbi: This glass of wine is symbolic of the cup of life. As you share this cup of wine, you share all that the future may bring.

[Rabbi pronounces the kiddush blessing in Hebrew—see page 70, no. 3, for a transliteration—and in English.]

Blessed art thou, O Lord our God, Creator of the Fruit of the Vine.

[Pam drinks.]

Minister: As you share from this cup, so may you draw contentment, comfort and happiness from your own cup of life. May you find life's joys heightened, its bitterness sweetened, and all things hallowed by true companionship and love.

[Larry drinks.]

FINAL BLESSING/PRONOUNCEMENT

Rabbi: Pam and Larry, now you will not know the cold, for you will be each warmth to the other. Now you will not know the dark, for you will be each light to the other. You have this day raised up a shelter against the loneliness of human existence. Though you are two bodies, there is but one life before you. May your years be good and long upon the earth, and may all that is beautiful and true abide with you forever.

Minister: Both [Rabbi] and I invoke upon you an ancient blessing taken from the Book of Numbers, a scripture from the Old Testament that we both hold mutually sacred:

[Rabbi and Minister alternate reading in Hebrew and in English, respectively. See page 70, no. 2, for transliteration of the Hebrew.]

May God be with you and help you to grow together.

May you enjoy the peace of home, of mind and of heart together.

May the Lord bless and keep you.

May the Lord cause his face to shine upon you and be gracious unto you.

May the Lord lift his countenance upon you and give you peace. Amen.

Rabbi: [Rabbi explains tradition of breaking the glass—see page 69 for some ideas.]

In conformity with ancient custom and according to the laws of the state of [state], I now pronounce you husband and wife.

[Larry breaks the glass and kisses Pam.]

RECESSIONAL

The Wedding of Kathryn and Lance / June 4, 1995
Officiated by a Minister and Rabbi

Processional

Opening Welcome

Minister

Opening Blessing

Rabbi   (For the Hebrew transliteration and English translation, see page 70, no. 1.)

Scriptural Readings

Lance's sister   Song of Songs 2:10-14

Kathryn's brother-in-law   1 John 3:18-22, 4:7-8

Statement of Intentions

Minister with Lance and Kathryn

Vows

Minister with Lance and Kathryn

Lance: Kathryn, I take you to be my wife from this time onward,

to join with you and to share all that is to come,

to give and to receive,

to speak and to listen,

to inspire and to respond,

and in all our life together to be loyal to you.

Kathryn: Lance, I take you to be my husband from this time onward,

to join with you and to share all that is to come,

to give and to receive,

to speak and to listen,

to inspire and to respond,

and in all our life together to be loyal to you.

Blessing of Rings

Rabbi

RING EXCHANGE

Rabbi with Lance and Kathryn

	[Lance places ring on Kathryn's finger.]
Lance:	(For several options for the Hebrew transliteration and English translation, see pp. 70-71, nos. 6–8.)
	This ring is a symbol that you have become my wife in the love of God.
Kathryn:	In accepting this ring, I pledge you all my love and devotion.
	[Kathryn places ring on Lance's finger.]
Kathryn:	This ring is a symbol that you have become my husband in the love of God.
Lance:	In accepting this ring, I pledge you all my love and devotion.

READING OF KETUBAH

Best Man	[Reads statement of marriage.]

PRESENTATION OF ROSES

Lance and Kathryn

[Roses are given to the mothers of bride and groom. See page 73 for an explanation of this tradition.]

WEDDING BLESSINGS AND SHARING OF WINE

Rabbi, Minister, and Guests

	[Rabbi recites all of the Hebrew blessings, alternating with guests who recite the English translations. Minister recites the English translation of final blessing.]
Guest 1:	You abound in blessings, Eternal our God, Source of all creation, Creator of the fruit of the vine.
Guest 2:	You abound in blessings Eternal our God, Source of all creation, all of whose creations reflect Your glory.
Guest 3:	You abound in blessings Eternal our God, Source of all creations, Creator of human beings.
Guest 4:	You abound in blessings, Eternal our God, Source of all creation, who created man and woman in Your image

Reflections from the groom:

We were lucky to find a good place to have our ceremony. My wife attends a United Methodist church that also rents the building to a Reform Jewish congregation. Both congregations use the fellowship hall for a sanctuary, and all of the religious symbols are easily removable. We had a large brass cross on a piano next to the huppah. Other than the items used in the wedding and the clothes worn by the officiants, there were no other religious trappings in the room. We did use the communion table to hold the props for the wedding (kiddush cup, etc.), although we turned it around so you couldn't see the writing on it.

We presented roses to each other's parents and made a statement thanking them for raising such a wonderful child and for accepting us as part of the family. We thought this was an important part of the ceremony.

The rabbi did the full, traditional blessings in Hebrew, but we used a more liberal English interpretation. We omitted the English verse about Zion. It worked well to have friends and family do the first blessings in English and the minister do the last one in English.

The rabbi explained the symbolism of the Jewish components in his homily (the huppah, breaking of the glass, etc.). He also gave a great little speech on marriage.

that they might live, love, and so perpetuate life. You abound in blessings, Eternal God, Creator of human beings.

Guest 5: Grant perfect joy to these loving companions, as You did to the first man and woman in the Garden of Eden. Praised are You, O Eternal, who grants the joy of bride and groom.

Minister: Praised are You, O Eternal our God, Ruler of the universe, who created joy and gladness, bride and groom, mirth, song, delight and rejoicing, love and harmony, peace and companionship. O Eternal our God, may there ever be heard in the cities of Judah and in the streets of Jerusalem voices of joy and gladness, voices of bride and groom, the jubilant voices of those joined in marriage under the bridal canopy, the voices of young people feasting and singing. Praised are You, O Eternal, who causes the groom to rejoice with his bride.

STATEMENT OF MARRIAGE

Minister: Since both of you have joined voluntarily in this ceremony which binds you together in marriage, abiding by the laws of the state of (state) and acting in accordance with the love of God, you, Lance (full name), and you, Kathryn (full name), are now husband and wife, man and woman united in marriage.

PRIESTLY BLESSING

Minister: May you be blessed with joy and gladness, vigor of body and spirit, love and harmony, companionship and love.

Rabbi: [Rabbi recites the Hebrew version of the following blessing. See page 70, no. 2, for a transliteration of the Hebrew.]

Minister: May God bless you, and guard you. May God show you favor, and be gracious to you. May God show you kindness and grant you peace. Amen.

HOMILY

Rabbi

BREAKING OF GLASS

Lance

RECESSIONAL

The Wedding of Karen and Dan / July 18, 1993
Officiated by a Priest and a Religious Scholar

This is an example of a wedding in which the Jewish presence was manifested, not by a rabbi, but by an individual knowledgeable about Jewish and Christian traditions and beliefs. In this case, the individual was an ordained lay minister who had been raised in an interfaith family. He is learned in Jewish, Catholic, and Protestant traditions and liturgy. You may find that, if you want your ceremony to include traditions from both of your religious backgrounds, and you cannot or choose not to have a rabbi present, you can draw on the talents of such a learned individual. [Note: in the following ceremony, the role of this religious scholar is marked by the word "Celebrant."]

Welcome

Priest: On behalf of Karen, Dan, and their families, we extend a warm welcome to all of you, and we are all elated that you could join us for this joyous marriage celebration.

(To the bride and groom)

We have come together this day to uphold you, Karen (full name), and you, Dan (full name), as you exchange your vows of marriage. We celebrate with you the love you have discovered in each other, and we support your decision to continue your life's journey together as husband and wife.

(To the congregation)

Karen and Dan came together from different backgrounds and experiences. Through their marriage they do not leave those behind but instead, form a new family that will broaden the circle of love and understanding in this world.

Celebrant: Whatever source of spiritual guidance you follow, when we strip all the opinions away, the central theme is that, whatever our religion, we are all one family.

With that in mind, Dan and Karen have asked us to perform this marital ritual of celebration with you—their immediate and extended family—by combining both of their individual spiritual traditions into this ceremony. As you will experience, the principles and sentiments of this ceremony will be very familiar to all of you.

Whenever the language of Hebrew is spoken, the English translation will follow.

Welcome Blessing

Celebrant: (See page 70, no. 4, for a transliteration of the Hebrew.)

Priest: Who is splendor over everything

Who is blessed over everything

Who is full of this abundance

Bless this groom and bride.

EXPLANATION OF HUPPAH

[Readings are done by the four people holding the poles of the huppah.]

Reader 1: Long after tents vanished from the Jewish landscape, wedding ceremonies were held out of doors in the hope that the marriage would be blessed by as many children as "the stars of the heavens." Some kind of covering was employed to create a more modest and sanctified space.

Reader 2: The bridal canopy, or huppah, is a multifaceted symbol. It symbolizes: modesty in the presence of God, the safety of your home, the protection of a garment, the intimacy of your bed covering.

Reader 3: It is open on all four sides—to respect Abraham, who had doors on all four sides of his home so that visitors would always know they were welcome.

Reader 4: The huppah does not promise that love or hope or pledges will keep out weather or catastrophe. But its few lines are a sketch for what might be. The flimsiness of the huppah is a reminder that the only thing that is real about a home is the people in it who love and choose to be together— to be a family. The only anchor that they will have will be holding onto each other's hands. The huppah is the house of promises. It is the home of hope.

PRAYER

Priest: We thank you, God, for granting us life and freedom, sustaining us in health, helping us prosper, and, in love, permitting us to reach this occasion together.

We thank You for all our blessings this day, and most especially, we thank You for the blessings of parenthood and children, for these are the blessings that allow us to be part of the great miracle of creation.

Eternal God, we ask Your continued blessing. Grant these, Your children, Karen and Dan, length of days, health, and happiness together. Endow them, we pray, with qualities of patience, understanding, and abundant love. If it be Your will, may they come to know the special joy and fulfilment of bringing their own children to the marriage ceremony. Amen.

MUSICAL INTERLUDE

PRESENTATION OF ROSES

Celebrant: Won't all of you please spend a few moments in silent prayer, to appreciate your own blessings of love and family, while Karen and Dan honor their own families.

[Karen and Dan give roses to each other's family.]

BLESSING OVER THE WINE

Celebrant: (See page 70, no. 3, for a transliteration of the Hebrew.)

Blessed art Thou, O Lord our God, King of the Universe, who created the fruit of the vine.

[Dan and Karen each take a sip of wine.]

Dan and Karen, as you have shared the wine of this cup, so may you, in God's presence, draw comfort, contentment, and felicity from the cup of life.

May you find life's joys heightened, its bitterness sweetened, and all things hallowed by true companionship, true understanding, and true love.

PRAYER

Celebrant: May you dare to dream dreams not yet dreamt.

May you find constant reward and challenge as you pursue the ongoing adventure of learning who you are and where you want to go.

May you always have a special sense of your mission in life together, and may you never tire of the endless possibilities of exploring your shared existence.

May God give you enough tension to keep you close to Him and each other, and enough joy to make you glad you have awakened to a new day.

May the winds that blow bring warmth enough to make you happy, but never enough to blow you apart; enough chill to keep you holding tightly to each other.

May God give you ears to hear each other, and more importantly, to hear His voice.

May He give you eyes to see each other smile, and to see the teardrop in the corner of one another's eye before it becomes a river, and may you have a keen sense of those times when the tenseness of the other's hand will cause you to hold on tightly to one another.

NEW TESTAMENT READING

Priest: I Corinthians 13

HOMILY

Priest: Karen and Dan, this wedding ceremony, of which you have been involved in the design, is by your intent both a celebration of your love for each other, and an exchange of commitments to each other.

You two are a good pairing. You complement each other. Your enjoyment of life together is more than it is when you are apart. With the love you have for each other, everything is possible.

Consequently, you think you should be married. All of us here today agree. We like the idea of you two together.

Karen and Dan, we live in a world where people ceaselessly deny the divine image implanted in them. To the degree that we continue to deny it, we bring about our own destruction, and the destruction not only of those we hate but also of those we love.

One of the most blatant denials of that image has been the enmity between Jews and Christians. There has been hatred and rancor and spite and almost everything else between Christians and Jews—almost everything else except love. Your marriage is a small and yet gigantic step in the reversal of that trend; for here you are, a Christian and a Jew, declaring in the most public and binding way your love for one another. That puts a special burden, and a special glory, upon your marriage. For your marriage becomes a sign, a very precious sign, that nothing—not even 2,000 years of enmity—is stronger than love.

So we thank you for that. You are already giving each of us a great gift—the gift of realizing that the love you affirm for each other also affirms the image of God in everyone; and so we too, through our love for one another, can affirm that image of God in ourselves. From the outside looking in, one could perceive your marriage as a tremendous challenge, given your different backgrounds. However, both of you choose to see it as an enrichment to both of your lives. I pray that throughout the whole of your marriage you can multiply to all who know you, a thousand-fold, the greatness of that gift.

You have told me that your intent is that this marriage be a lifetime arrangement. Who wouldn't want that? Yet, this is not so easy to attain these days. How is it that this marriage can last? A good deal of the answer lies in the love celebrated and the commitment shared today between you both.

You see, love and commitment are a good pairing as well. They also complement each other. They mean more together than they do apart. It seems anymore that love is like a Colorado thunderstorm. It falls on us without warning, and then slips away when we aren't paying attention. Surely your love for each other can have more endurance than that. The key lies in love, reinforced with commitment.

So Karen and Dan, always be scheming, just like adventurous children, to continually let one another know that each of you is the most important person in one another's life, and that your partner is truly loved.

May the love we celebrate, and the commitment you share, endure testing, and enrich with age. May you grow old together.

(Portions of this homily come from the work of theologian Robert McAfee Brown, of the Pacific School of Theology, in Berkeley, California.)

INTENTIONS

Celebrant:	(To the Groom)

Dan, the woman who stands by your side is about to become your wife. She will look to you for gentleness, for support, for understanding, for encouragement, and for protection. You must never take Karen for granted, but be continually sensitive to her needs. Your life and love will be Karen's greatest source of joy.

So I ask you, Dan, will you have Karen to be your lawfully wedded wife? Will you love her, and cherish her? Will you always uphold her and encourage her? Will you be loyal to her, and true? Will you honor her all her days, and be respectful of her, and will you promise to always bestow upon her your heart's deepest devotion? Will you?

Dan:	I will.
Priest:	(To the Bride)

Karen, the man who stands by your side is about to become your husband. He will look to you for gentleness, for support, for understanding, for protection and encouragement. You must never take Dan for granted, but be continually sensitive to his needs. Your life and love will be Dan's greatest source of joy.

So I ask you Karen, will you have Dan to be your lawfully wedded husband? Will you love him, and cherish him? Will you always uphold him and encourage him? Will you be loyal to him, and true? Will you honor him all his days, and be respectful of him? And will you promise to always bestow upon him your heart's deepest devotion? Will you?

Karen: I will.

CONGREGATIONAL ENVISIONMENT

Priest: (To the Guests)

Please stand.

If each of you here today celebrates with Dan and Karen the love they have discovered in each other, and if you commit to support their decision to marry by offering constant love, strengthening them by your wisest counsel (but only when it is requested), encouraging them by your thoughtful concern, and instructing them by your good example, please let Dan and Karen know your commitment by expressing your sentiments with a heartfelt "Amen!"

[Guests respond "Amen!"]

Priest: You may be seated.

MARRIAGE VOWS

Priest: (To the Groom)

With those intentions offered, please turn to each other, take one another's hand, and Dan, repeat after me:

I, Dan, take you, Karen, to be my wife, my friend, my love, and my lifelong companion: to share my life with yours. To build our dreams together, while allowing you to grow with your dreams; to support you through times of trouble, and rejoice with you in times of happiness; to treat you with respect, love, and loyalty through all the trials and triumphs of our lives together: and to give you, Karen, all the love I can give my whole life long. This commitment is made in love, kept in faith, lived in hope, and eternally made new.

[Dan repeats vow.]

Celebrant: (To the Bride)

And now, Karen, please repeat after me:

I, Karen, take you, Dan, to be my husband, my friend, my love, and my lifelong companion; to share my life with yours. To build our dreams together, while allowing you to grow with your dreams; to support you through times of trouble, and rejoice with you in times of happiness; to treat you with respect, love, and loyalty through all the trials and triumphs of our lives together: and to give you, Dan, all the love I can give my whole life long. This commitment is made in love, kept in faith, lived in hope, and eternally made new.

[Karen repeats vow.]

BLESSING OVER THE RINGS

Celebrant: These rings are the symbols of the vows here taken; circles of wholeness; endless in form. These rings mark the beginning of a long journey together for both of you; a journey filled with wonder, surprises, laughter, tears, celebration, discovery, and joy.

So let us bless these rings with these words from Black Elk, a Sioux Indian Holy Man:

Everything the 'power of the world' does, is done in a circle.

The sky is round, and I have heard that the earth is round like a ball, and so are the stars.

The wind, in its greatest power, whirls.

Birds make their nests in circles, for theirs is the same religion as ours.

The sun comes forth and goes down again in a circle.

Even the seasons form a great circle in their changing, and always come back again to where they were.

Life is a circle from childhood to childhood.

So it is in everything where power moves.

RING CEREMONY—BETROTHAL

Celebrant: (To the Groom)

And so, Dan, I will ask you now to take this ring of gold, place it on Karen's left ring finger, and say with me this ancient marriage vow, which I will give to you word by word, first in Hebrew, then in English:

(See page 70, no. 6, for a transliteration of the Hebrew.)

By this ring, as a token and pledge of my constant love, you are consecrated to me as my wedded wife.

[Dan repeats vow.]

Priest: (To the Bride)

And Karen, will you, in turn, take this ring of gold, place it upon Dan's left ring finger and say after me:

(See page 70, no. 6, for a transliteration of the Hebrew.)

By this ring, as a token and pledge of my constant love, you are consecrated to me as my wedded husband.

[Karen repeats vow.]

Priest: And so it is.

May your rings always be the symbols of the unbroken circle of love.

Love freely given has no beginning and no end.

May your rings always call to mind the freedom and the power of this love.

[Karen and Dan lay their palms up as Priest and Celebrant support their hands.]

May these rings now on your fingers symbolize to you and all who know you, not only the vows of marriage you have made here this day, but also the infinite touch of God—that which is magnified and sanctified and manifested in the love you carry in your hearts. Hold fast to that love and keep its light shining brightly all the days of your lives.

PRONOUNCEMENT

Priest: Karen and Dan, you both have joined voluntarily in this ceremony of marriage, and have been formally united as husband and wife in the presence of your family and community.

Celebrant: And as you have declared openly your clear intention to be considered before all the world as a married couple, and have exchanged rings and vows attesting thereto, it is our distinct pleasure to declare you now, and before God and these witnesses, to be husband and wife.

KISS I

Priest: The universe hangs on a kiss, exists in the hold of a kiss.

You may kiss.

BENEDICTION

Priest: May the road rise to meet you

May the wind be ever at your back

May the good Lord ever keep you

In the hollow of his hand

May your hearts be warm as your hearthstone

And may God bless you always.

OLD TESTAMENT BENEDICTION

[Celebrant and Priest alternate Hebrew and English. See page 70, no. 2, for a transliteration of the Hebrew.]

Priest: May the Lord bless you and keep you.

May the Lord's face shine on you and be gracious to you.

May the Lord look upon you with favor, and give you peace. Amen.

EXPLANATION OF THE BREAKING OF THE GLASS

Celebrant: Breaking a glass reminds us that although the wedding has provided joy, the broken world still requires our attention, and people less fortunate still require our care. Its breaking is not only a reminder of sorrow, but also an expression of hope for a future free from all violence.

Frailty of the glass also suggests the frailty of human relationships. Even the strongest love is subject to disintegration. The glass, then, is broken to "protect" the marriage with an implied prayer, "As this glass shatters, so may our marriage never break."

BREAKING OF THE GLASS

[Both Karen and Dan step on the glass.]

KISS II

[The Congregation yells "Mazel Tov." Karen and Dan kiss.]

INTRODUCTION

Priest: Will everyone please stand?

Good family and friends, it is our honor to present to you, for the first time, Dan (full name) and Karen (full name), a married couple.

RECESSIONAL

INTIMACY

"Intimacy" means arranging for a few minutes alone with each other immediately after the wedding ceremony. This has been found by countless couples to be one of the most memorable, precious moments together on their wedding day. Arrange for a private place where you retire alone after you've left the ceremony—you are the first ones to leave, after all. Ask your best man to arrange for a bit of food and libation to be available in your private room. Plan this time for between 15 and 20 minutes; then, refreshed and connected, you can join your guests. But be warned, one couple enjoyed this "intimacy" time so much, they took more than an hour alone!

RECEPTION

Karen and Dan turn and face their guests for the first time as married partners.

The Wedding of Patricia and David / July 18, 1987
Officiated by a Priest and a Rabbi

"Two persons who love each other are in a place more holy than a temple or church."

William Phelps

Prelude

"Jesu, Joy of Man's Desiring" / Bach

Traditional Shaker Melody, from "Appalachian Spring" / Copland

Medley to our Grandparents: A salute through the music of their countries of origin

Hungarian:	Hungarian Dance #4 / Brahms
Irish:	"Londonderry Air" (also known as "Danny Boy")
German:	"Singer's Joy Polka" / Johann Strauss
Viennese:	"Vienna Life" / Johann Strauss
Russian:	"Dark Eyes" / Traditional
Repeat:	"Danny Boy"

Processional

Canon in D / Pachelbel

Opening Statements by Priest and Rabbi

[The clergy address the following points in their own words:

Welcome. Patty and David have designed this ceremony to reflect the traditions of both faiths. The couple feels strongly that their two faiths are mutually enhancing, not mutually exclusive. Patty and David see Judaism and Catholicism as two parts of the same circle, with God at the center. Patty and David are mutually devoted to each of their families—and could not be doing this without their strength and support. They are integral to this ceremony.]

Lighting of the Unity Candles
and Statements by Parents

[Priest explains the significance of the Unity Candle. There is a blue taper for David's parents to light, and a white one for Patty's parents. Patty and David will light a blue and white havdalah candle. David's parents, Judy and Lou, read their personal statements and light their candle.]

Reflections from the couple:

We were very fortunate that a number of wonderful things happened to make our wedding ceremony everything we wanted and more. We had the love and support of both of our families. Patty grew up in the suburban Cincinnati area, where there were a number of rabbis who were willing to officiate (Cincinnati is the home of Hebrew Union College–Jewish Institute of Religion, the Rabbinical College of Reform Judaism).

We were able to write a ceremony that we felt to be expressive of not only our marriage vows, but also the spiritual life we planned to lead together. Since we both come from a background in theater (writing and acting), this was an exciting opportunity for us. Including our parents' personal statements (and our own) seemed fitting to the idea of creating our own ceremony, but we didn't realize how surprising and fulfilling these spoken words would turn out to be. The most powerful moment of the ceremony was when David (the Jewish partner) led the guests in the Lord's Prayer and Patty (the Christian) did the same with the Sh'ma. By reciting the central prayers of our two faiths, we were able to make the statement that we embraced each others' faiths as well as each other.

(continued on page 53)

Judy: Parents cannot protect a child from the hurts that come in life. But we pray that we can give you a safe place while you are with us, so that you can learn to grow in wisdom and in strength. Then you can move on, to use that wisdom and strength to become the loving man you are, David.

And now you and Patty commit to share your lives. What follows is the product of the strengths of both of you, matched in love and values. As you create your new family, we watch with love and joy.

Lou: I hope someday

My son will say

He sent his child on his way

Without a fear

Without a doubt

Of knowing what his life's about.

I know I can today.

[Patty's parents, Lorraine and Dick, read their personal statements and light their candle.]

Lorraine: Sixty-one years ago today, my mother brought me into the world. She cared for me with love, wisdom, discipline, sweetness and light.

She left behind bequests to me which I gave to you during your formative years, and I hope that you will in turn pass these on to your children...

One is roots...

The other is wings!

Dick: The greatest gift that anyone can give is part of one's self. Lorraine and I are giving such a gift today. We are giving you a priceless part of our family treasure, an irreplaceable part of ourselves.

So, David, we ask you to accept this, our gift, with the gentleness, the kindness, the love which we have always tried to give her during her life with us. May you help her to achieve the happiness and the fulfillment which she so fervently desires.

And you, Patty, are today receiving a similar gift from Judy and Lou. Nurture and care for him as lovingly and unselfishly as you are capable of doing. In your lifetime I know you have seen some examples of unselfish love—love that expects nothing in return. It means not giving 50%, but 100% of yourself, even though at times you may feel it is not expressly appreciated or returned. True love is its own reward.

So, David and Patty, may your lives together be so happy and fulfilling that after many fruitful years, we may all meet in that heaven to which we all aspire, and you may say to us:

Here is your treasure, not only untarnished, but actually glistening more brilliantly that when it was given. We have fulfilled the deep trust which you have placed in us on our wedding day.

Shalom. God Bless You!

READING

Sonnet 116 / Shakespeare

Guest: [Read with musical accompaniment.]

Let me not to the marriage of true minds

Admit impediments. Love is not love

Which alters when it alteration finds

Or bends with the remover to remove;

Oh, no! It is an ever-fixed mark,

That looks on tempests and is never shaken;

It is the star to every wandering bark,

Whose worth unknown, although his height be taken.

Love's not time's fool. Though rosy lips and cheeks

Within his bending sickle compass come;

Love alters not with his brief hours and weeks,

But blows it out even to the edge of doom.

If this be error and upon me proved,

I never writ, nor no man ever loved.

(continued from page 51)

The reactions of the guests after the wedding were as amazing. The nun who had been Patty's mentor in high school complemented her on her Hebrew. Her father, it turned out, was a Jew. Friends of Patty's parents told us: "This was the wedding we wanted to have 30 years ago but couldn't." Interfaith weddings, especially in that area, were unheard of then. In fact, this was the first time this particular priest had ever performed one.

Along with the days of the births of our two children, this was the happiest day of our life. It is a joy to share it with you.

MUSICAL INTERLUDE

"Sabbath Prayer"/ J. Bock and S. Harnick

INVOCATION TO BRING GOD INTO CEREMONY

Priest

READING FROM OLD TESTAMENT

Rabbi: Song of Solomon 2:1-14, 16

(This passage was selected because it draws the parallel between the love of God and the love of a man and a woman. It also demonstrates the nature of true love, especially two individuals who waited for so long to find someone who could show what Love means.)

RESPONSORIAL PSALM

Rabbi: Psalm 19 [with string accompaniment]

READING FROM NEW TESTAMENT

Priest: I Corinthians 12:31 and 13:1-13

(This passage was selected because it expresses the necessity of love in order to be fully human.)

A Reading for the Children in Attendance

The Children in the Wedding Party:

[a passage from *The Velveteen Rabbit* by Margery Williams, with musical accompaniment]

Homily

Rabbi

Personal Statements by Bride and Groom

David: I don't know why marriage is called "settling down."

I think of it as "settling up."

A reconciliation...

An ending and a beginning...

The most important transition of my life.

A step I take with joy...

Because at last

I've become settled with myself.

I look ahead with anticipation.

Together, we will write an epic.

One with many episodes...hundreds of characters...

a plot with many twists and turns...

continuously unfolding.

We are the protagonists—volitional...

Three dimensional characters...roles that any actor would relish.

We're ready to fight to the death for what we hold precious.

And God is writing our story.

How will it all turn out?

Knowing that would kind of spoil it.

All I know is that a life lived well will test us—challenge us—

and ultimately reward us.

I know I have weaknesses, my love.

But we are a team.

You help me turn my weakness into strength.

I want you by my side—always.

As we look ahead—and imagine the adventures to come—

I know that I have the best possible partner in the world.

So let it begin!

I am ready!

Patty: I am not Cinderella; you are not Prince Charming. I am not a damsel in distress; you wear no shining armor. Yet you are the knight who broke down my armor, that wall of defense to arm my vulnerable self against the ravages of hollowness, loneliness and isolation. You melted metal with sincerity, patience, intelligence, wit, selflessness—your goodness. You waged not a sudden attack, but an effortless, steady pursuit. We took time. You waited, I did not retreat.

I have looked *into* your eyes and have seen that you perceive the truest Patty, so wise, so emotional, so multi-faceted. You celebrate my strengths and tolerate my foibles.

I have looked *through* your eyes and have seen that the true David is so genuine, so gentle, so full of humanity. I cherish your strengths and smile at your foibles.

I have looked *beyond* your eyes and have glimpsed that love of God, for the love of a man and a woman is but a fraction of God's love. I recognize His strength and honor His power.

I have looked *with* our eyes and have seen a future that must be spent with you and, hopefully, our children. You are my equal and my balance, the "Thou" for my "I," my partner, my life's enhancer. And I have discovered that this is love.

I no longer see with the starry eyes of youth. You have awakened me with your kiss, but life is not a fairy tale. It is an adventure. I set forth today on the greatest human adventure. As your wife, I am ready to look into, through and beyond your eyes for a lifetime. For life without those eyes would be blind indeed.

Vows

Priest: Patty and David, have you come here freely and without reservation to give yourselves to each other in marriage?

**Patty
and David:**   We have.

Priest: Will you love and honor each other as man and wife for the rest of your lives?

**Patty
and David:**   We will.

Priest: Will you accept children lovingly from God and bring them up according to His Law?

**Patty
and David:**   We will.

Priest: Since it is your intention to enter into the marriage, join your right hands and declare your consent before God.

David: I, David, take you, Patty, to be my wife. I promise to be true to you in good times and in bad, in sickness and in health. I will love you and honor you all the days of my life.

Patty:	I, Patty, take you, David, to be my husband. I promise to be true to you in good times and in bad, in sickness and in health. I will love you and honor you all the days of my life.

BLESSING OVER THE RINGS

Priest:	Lord, bless and consecrate Patty and David in their love for each other. May these rings be a symbol of true faith in each other, and always remind them of their love.
Rabbi:	As you, David, place this ring on Patty's finger, say unto her these words: With this ring, be thou consecrated unto me as my wife, in everlasting love.

[**David repeats pledge.**]

And you, Patty, place this ring upon David's finger as a token of wedlock and say to him these words: With this ring, be thou consecrated unto me as my husband, in everlasting love.

[**Patty repeats pledge.**]

In keeping with the declaration you have made, you have given and received these rings. They are a token of your union, a symbol of enduring love. May they ever remind you that your lives are to be bound together by devotion and faithfulness.

(See page 70, no. 5, for a transliteration of the Hebrew.)

Blessed art Thou, O Lord our God, who sanctifies Thy people by the covenant of marriage.

LIGHTING OF THE UNITY CANDLE BY BRIDE AND GROOM

Priest:	This candle, too, is a symbol of a life of sharing. As you light this taper, remember that you are still two individuals, but you now share one life. True love consists not of gazing only at each other, but in gazing outward together in the same direction.

MUSICAL INTERLUDE

"Ave Maria" / Schubert

PRAYERS OF THE FAITHFUL

[After each prayer, the congregation responds: "Lord, hear our prayer."]

Priest:	For Patty and David, that the love and joy we celebrate with them today will be continuously renewed throughout their lifetimes.
Rabbi:	For the families, that their love, understanding and support will enrich the marriage of Patty and David, and that their union will be a lifelong blessing to their families.
Maid of Honor:	For the children, that their innocence, joy, and unquestioning love—their smiles and laughter will help Patty and David to remember always what is real.
Best Man:	For the faith, the hope and the love we see exemplified today in the union of Patty and David, so that those virtues may be shared by those gathered and carried with us all our days.
David:	For Father (name) and Rabbi (name), in appreciation for their kindness, guidance and blessings in making our ceremony an enrichment of our love.

Patty: For our dear and close family and friends, who have come to share our joy on the most meaningful day of our lives.

[**After the last response, Patty says:**]

If anyone in the congregation would like to share their thoughts with us and with God, please do so.

STATEMENTS FROM THE COMMUNITY

[Guests stand and speak to the bride and groom.]

THE SEVEN WEDDING BLESSINGS

Rabbi: [The blessings are chanted or spoken first in Hebrew, then in English.]

HANDSHAKE OF PEACE

Priest: [Priest asks the congregation to share with one another a visual sign of God's peace and love. Musical accompaniment: "Prayer of St. Francis"]

Lord, make me an instrument of your peace.

Where there is hatred, let me sow love;

Where there is injury, pardon;

Where there is doubt, faith;

Where there is despair, hope;

Where there is darkness, light;

And where there is sadness, joy.

O Divine Master, grant that I may not so much seek

to be consoled as to console;

to be understood as to understand;

to be loved as to love.

For it is in giving that we receive,

it is in pardoning that we are pardoned, and

it is in dying that we are born to eternal life.

BLESSING OVER THE WINE

Rabbi: [Rabbi announces that the wine to be used was made by Patty's father and more will be available at the reception.]

This cup of wine is symbolic of the cup of life. As you share the one cup of wine, you undertake to share all that the future may bring.

(See page 70, no. 3, for a transliteration of the Hebrew.)

Blessed art Thou, O Lord our God, King of the Universe, who has created the fruit of the vine.

CONCLUDING PRAYERS

The Lord's Prayer and The Sh'ma

David: Please rise.

A reading from the Book of Luke, Chapter 11.

And it came to pass that as He was praying in a certain place, and when He ceased, one of His disciples said unto Him, "Lord, teach us to pray, as John also taught his disciples." And He said unto them, "When you pray, say

Our Father, which art in Heaven, hallowed be thy name. Thy kingdom come, thy will be done, on earth as it is in Heaven. Give us this day our daily bread, and forgive us our trespasses, as we forgive those who trespass against us. And lead us not into temptation, but deliver us from evil. For thine is the kingdom, and the power and the glory, forever." Amen.

Patty: (in Hebrew and in English)

Hear O Israel, the Lord is our God, the Lord is One.

Blessed is his glorious kingdom for ever and ever!

Rabbi: [Says the rest of the Sh'ma in Hebrew.]

Patty and David: You shall love the Lord your God with all your mind, with all your strength, and with all your being. Set these words, which I command you this day, upon your heart. Teach them faithfully to your children, speak of them in your home and on your way, when you lie down and when you rise up. Bind them as a sign upon your hand; let them be a symbol before your eyes; inscribe them on the doorposts of your house, and upon your gates.

Rabbi: [Continues in Hebrew]

Patty and David: Be mindful of all my Mitzvot and do them: so shall you consecrate yourself to your God. I the Lord am your God who led you out of Egypt to be your God. I the Lord am your God.

BREAKING OF THE GLASS

Rabbi: [Gives some of the various reasons behind the tradition of the breaking of the glass. See page 69 for some explanations for this tradition. David breaks glass.]

RECESSIONAL

"Eine Kleine Nachtmusik" / Mozart

"Ode to Joy" / Beethoven

CHAPTER FIVE

SELECTED EXCERPTS FROM OTHER CEREMONIES

As interfaith wedding ceremonies were compiled and reviewed to create this book, it was striking how many couples chose to use very similar readings, scriptural passages, musical selections, and rituals. For example, many of the collected ceremonies include readings from the standard wedding scriptures: the love ballads in Song of Songs and the definition of love in First Corinthians (chapters 12 and 13). But many couples also choose to incorporate a reading with special meaning for interfaith families from the book of Ruth (1:15–18). This passage describes how Ruth casts her lot with her new religion and her new family, saying, "wherever you go, I will go; wherever you live, I will live. Your people will be my people, and your God will be my God."

Many interfaith couples choose to incorporate the symbolism of the unity candle into their ceremonies. By asking their parents or other family members to light two distinct and separate candles, and then lighting a central candle (sometimes with two wicks) from each of the family candles, a couple can convey graphically their desire to join two separate families and two separate religions in one household.

The "Recognition of Family and Guests" part of your ceremony can be an important way to make family feel included and even vested in your wedding. You can incorporate aspects of giving and receiving—giving roses or other recognition to your two families, and receiving affirmation from them of their continuing commitment to supporting you, individually and as a couple.

> **What then is very important is your investment in the *form* of your wedding. Spending as much time in its preparation as you do for the ancillary activities such as place, food, band and photographer has a way of paying off in huge emotional dividends. You honor your relationship by the way in which you lovingly express your commitment in the presence of family and friends. It is about your love—what it means to you, where you want it to take you, and what hopes you have for it.**
>
> **— Rabbi Allen Secher**

Interfaith couples often ask their officiant to speak directly to their special situation in his or her welcome or remarks. Replete with honesty, sensitivity and optimism, these speeches frequently turn out to be the most emotional moment of the wedding ceremony. A couple's vows as well can be an opportunity for the bride and groom to state clearly what they believe about their love and their interfaith relationship.

Most interfaith couples choose to incorporate some clearly Jewish traditions. Almost every interfaith wedding ceremony we've seen includes the sharing of wine and the breaking of the glass at the end. This certainly doesn't mean that you have to do these things, just that they seem to convey an attachment to Judaism that is very often important to the Jewish partner in an interfaith couple.

As you review the selected excerpts on the following pages, try to imagine how they would fit into your vision of your wedding day. Some will feel right, some will not fit what you and your partner want to convey. You may want to insert some of these selections into one of the sample ceremonies in the preceding chapter.

Trust your emotional responses—only the two of you can create the ceremony the way you want it. And feel free to cross out words and rewrite sections to fit your own thoughts and desires for your ceremony more perfectly. After all, it's your day!

WELCOMES

Pastor: It is one of life's richest surprises when the accidental meeting of two life paths leads them to proceed together along the common path of husband and wife. It is indeed one of life's finest experiences when a casual relationship grows into a permanent bond of love. This meeting and this growing brings us together today.

Rabbi: In the presence of God, we come to join [Bride] and [Groom] in marriage. It is fitting and appropriate that you, their family and friends, witness and participate in their wedding. For the ideals, the understanding, and the mutual respect which they bring to their marriage have their roots in the love, friendship and guidance you have given them.

May theirs then always be a shared adventure, rich with moments of serenity, as well as excitement; vital with problems that test, as well as successes that lift; marked by a sense of personal freedom, as well as mutual responsibility.

[Bride] and [Groom], you have asked both [Pastor] and me to participate in the ceremony that unites you and to witness your exchange of vows. In doing so you are asking us to join you in expressing to your family and friends the fact that each of you considers your religious upbringing and tradition to be important. In marriage you choose not to sacrifice your commitment to your heritage but instead to share it with one another and with your children in the years ahead.

Welcome and thank you for being here. Today's ceremony witnesses the union of two people, two families, two traditions. We have deliberately incorporated elements of both traditions that are meaningful to us. Not completely Jewish or Christian, this ceremony is our own personal attempt to share our vision of the commitment we are making to each other.

INVOCATIONS

Priest: Let us pray:

In this sacred hour, and at this special moment in time, we open our hearts in prayer on behalf of [Bride] and [Groom].

Gracious God, you have made the bond of marriage a holy mystery. With faith in you and in each other, [Groom] and [Bride] pledge their love today. May their lives always bear witness to the reality of that love.

Amen.

Rabbi: May they share their experiences and their feelings with one another and thereby find life's deepest meaning and richest happiness.

May the covenant which [Bride] and [Groom] now seal always be blessed with truth and devotion.

And may their lives be bound together in understanding and with intimacy so to treasure all of life's experiences by sharing them always in love.

Amen.

....

Pastor: Today we are privileged to share with [Groom] and [Bride] a moment of supreme joy in the new life they now begin together. It is not our hour of exultation, but theirs. Yet would we speak our hopes for them. In the years ahead may their wisdom be increased, that they may always apply tenderness and strength to the trials which will surely befall them. May they never allow changing customs and fashions to dull the sense of loyal love and utter devotion now theirs. When new lives are added to the fellowship that is their home, may they give thanks for the blessing of a child, and bring it to the fullness of its promise by the same light of love which now glows in them. And may they look beyond the limits of their own existence to the larger family of man, realizing its just claim upon them. For no marriage ought to be celebrated, nor none fulfilled, unless a portion of its end be directed toward the enoblement of all mankind.

CANDLE LIGHTING

Priest: The light of these candles represents the warmth and fragility of love. As you light this single candle from your separate candles, let us reflect on the significance today. Prior to this moment, you each walked a separate path. Now, as you light this candle, you embark together on a shared path.

[Light the candle. Musical interlude. Sign of peace by priest.]

....

Officiant: [Couple provides three candles and a pair of candlesticks to symbolize the beginning of a new family and home that will be filled with light. Two family members or attendants light one candle each. The officiant reads the following as the candles are lighted.]

The Ba'al Shem Tov said: "From every human being there rises a light that reaches straight to heaven. When two souls that are destined for each other find one another, their streams of light flow together and a single brighter light goes forth from their united being." In this spirit, [Groom] and [Bride], take your individual candles and light together a third candle which symbolizes your marital bond.

....

Rabbi: With flames taken from the candles their parents lit, [Bride] and [Groom] light one candle together. Their candle is one unit with two wicks, symbolizing that even in unity they can remain individuals. They will become one family, but each brings uniqueness to their union.

RECOGNITION OF FAMILY AND GUESTS

Groom: We thank everyone for coming today. Your presence makes this ceremony more meaningful for us.

Bride:	We especially want to thank our parents—not just for being here today, but for being there for us so many times in the past.
Groom:	We learned how to love because we were raised in loving homes.
Bride:	We feel secure and confident in our love because our parents allowed us to be independent. They are the wind beneath our wings.
Groom:	They have shown us, by example, what a happy marriage can be.
Bride:	Although we are founding a new home, the love we feel for the homes of our childhood will continue.
Officiant:	As they come before us to be married, [Groom] and [Bride] wish to acknowledge and thank [Bride's parents' names] and [Groom's parents' names] for the love and support they have given them. The flowers they give to their parents represent feelings of gratitude in the hearts of [Bride] and [Groom]. This moment marks a major change in their lives, but the ties of love and friendship with their parents will continue.
	[The bride and groom then walk to their parents, who rise, and the bride and groom hug each of them and give each a rose.]
	[Groom] and [Bride], as you share a rose with your parents, let this be a symbol of your love for each other's relatives. Marriage is more than simply the joining of two lives. It is the marriage of two families. May your love for them, as well as their love for you, live on, by God's grace.
Pastor:	[If a parent or other family member chooses not to be with you on your wedding day, you can acknowledge this person's importance to you by saying the following.]
	As [Bride] and [Groom] are joining together to create a new family today, they also wish to send their blessings and love to those who are unable to be here today: [list name(s) of those who aren't present].
Officiant:	Will the parents of [Bride] and [Groom] please rise, and before God and all who are gathered here, affirm your blessings, support and encouragement. I remind you that, although each of them will remain a part of your separate heritage, they are no longer your separate children. [Bride] and [Groom] are here, before Almighty God, to become one. Therefore, I now ask you: do you offer your blessings and loving support of this marriage?
Parents:	We do.
Officiant:	I now ask everyone to rise. Do all of you gathered here today also pledge your support and encouragement for the commitment that [Groom] and [Bride] have made to one another? If so you pledge, would each of you respond by saying, "I do."
Congregation:	I do.

Officiant:	(To the Guests)
	Please stand. All of us who have come here today to celebrate with [Bride] and [Groom] comprise this couple's community. I invite each of you to offer your prayers silently as witness to your commitment to participate with joy in their life together.
	Promise your positive involvement and support of [Groom] and [Bride] to encourage the fulfillment of their dreams and to support their growth together; to uphold them and their family in their marriage; to support them in times of triumph and in times of strife; and to strive, each in your own way, to help them achieve a lifetime of happiness and fulfillment together.
	I ask your affirmation of all these for [Groom] and [Bride] by saying with me, Amen.
	[Guests respond, "Amen."]
	Thank you. You may be seated.

Vows

Groom:	I, [Groom], take you, [Bride], with all my heart and soul, to be my wife, my friend, my love, and my lifelong companion. I promise to respect that our ideas and opinions may differ, and to remember that yours hold as much truth and value for you as mine do for me. I promise to support you in times of trouble, and celebrate with you in times of happiness; to care more about your feelings than about being right, and to always listen without judging. I promise to treat you with respect, love, and loyalty through all the trials and triumphs of our lives together; and to give you, [Bride], all the love I can give, my whole life long. This commitment is made in love, kept in faith, lived in hope, and eternally made new.
Bride:	I, [Bride], take you, [Groom], with all my heart and soul, to be my husband, my friend, my love, and my lifelong companion. I promise to respect that our ideas and opinions may differ, and to remember that yours hold as much truth and value for you as mine do for me. I promise to support you in times of trouble, and celebrate with you in times of happiness; to care more about your feelings than about being right, and to always listen without judging. I promise to treat you with respect, love, and loyalty through all the trials and triumphs of our lives together; and to give you, [Groom], all the love I can give, my whole life long. This commitment is made in love, kept in faith, lived in hope, and eternally made new.
Groom:	In the presence of God and our friends, I, [Groom], take thee, [Bride], to be my beloved wife. Entreat me not to leave thee, or to return from following after thee. For whither thou goest I will go; and where thou lodgest, I will lodge. Thy people shall be my people, thy history, my history; and thy future, my future. In sickness and in health, in success and in failure, in joy and in sorrow, I trust you to care for our family. And I give you my faith and my love, in God's holy name.
Bride:	In the presence of God and our friends, I, [Bride], take thee, [Groom], to be my beloved husband. Entreat me not to leave thee, or to return from following after thee. For whither thou goest I will go; and where thou lodgest, I will lodge. Thy people shall be my people, thy history, my history; and thy future, my future. In sickness and in health, in success and in failure, in joy and in sorrow, I trust you to care for our family. And I give you my faith and my love, in God's holy name.

Bride,	
then Groom:	I believe in the power of love. I believe that love is the single most potent force in the universe. It is the source of all joy, the unifying strength which links spirit to spirit. The capacity to love is our great chance for happiness. On this wonderful day, my heart overflows with feelings of love. I love my family and friends; I love all of the people who came to witness this wedding. Most of all, I love you, [Name]. I believe so strongly in love's great power that I now promise to spend the rest of my lifetime with you.
Minister:	The hand offered by each of you is an extension of self, just as is your mutual love. Cherish the touch, for you touch not only your own, but another life. Be ever sensitive to its pulse. Seek always to understand and respect its rhythm. [Groom], do you take [Bride], in all her gentleness and sensitivity, for her warm heart and her understanding of you and your philosophy, for her search for truth and goodness, and her recognition of falseness and evil, and for her courage to embark along new and untried paths as conscience and necessity demand?
Groom:	Yes, I take her not only for these, but also in laughter and tears, in health and illness, in success and failure, in conflict and tranquility, in doubt and trust, as my wife and equal. Let this ring be a symbol of my vow.
Minister:	[Bride], do you take [Groom] for his discernment of truth in the face of discouragement, his pursuit of a simple life, his strength to follow the course his judgement dictates, and his deep love of his fellowman?
Bride:	Yes, I take him not only for these, but also in laughter and tears, in health and illness, in success and failure, in conflict and tranquility, in doubt and trust, as my husband and equal. Let this ring be a symbol of my vow.
Pastor:	It is most beautiful when two souls finally realize that marriage is the crown their love must wear, when each one is ready to say to the other: "I need you. I feel my life would be incomplete without you. I know that my happiness depends on how I strive to make you happy."
Groom,	
then Bride:	I pledge you my love, and whatever comforting, whatever care and aid and good company a husband/wife can give his/her wife/husband. I will live with you and honor you from this day forward. I will seek to know you well, and cherish all that concerns you. I will be with you, go with you, stay with you, and I will give thanks for our love.
Rabbi:	Do you, [Groom], take [Bride] to be your wife, promising to cherish and protect her, whether in good fortune or in adversity, and to seek together a life hallowed by the faith of humankind?
Groom:	I do.
Rabbi:	Do you, [Bride], take [Groom] to be your husband, promising to cherish and protect him, whether in good fortune or in adversity, and to seek together a life hallowed by the faith of humankind?

Bride: I do.

. . . .

**Groom,
then Bride:** I, [name], choose you, [name], to be my wife/husband, my friend, and my lover; to love, respect, and trust you; to support you and help you grow; to share my life with you forever as together we work to improve this world for our brothers and sisters and for our children.

EXCHANGE OF RINGS

Groom: (upon placing the ring on bride's finger)

Wherever you go, I will go:

wherever you live, I will live.

Your people shall be my people,

and your God, my God.

Wherever you die, I will die

and there I will be buried

May the lord do so to me

and more also

if even death should come between us!

Bride: (upon placing the ring on groom's finger)

Wherever you go, I will go:

wherever you live, I will live.

Your people shall be my people,

and your God, my God.

Wherever you die, I will die

and there I will be buried

May the lord do so to me

and more also

if even death should come between us!

from Ruth 1:16-18

. . . .

Officiant: From the earliest times, the circle has been a symbol of completeness, a symbol of committed love. An unbroken and never-ending circle symbolizes a commitment of love that is also never ending. These rings represent the ties that bind you together as husband and wife. They are made of gold, a metal that does not tarnish and is enduring. As often as either of you looks at these rings, I hope that you will be reminded of the enduring commitment to love each other which you have made today.

Will each of you repeat after me:

Groom: I, [Groom], give to you, [Bride], this ring, as a symbol of my commitment to love, honor, and respect you.

. . . .

| **Bride:** | I, [Bride], give to you, [Groom], this ring, as a symbol of my commitment to love, honor, and respect you. |

BLESSING OVER THE WINE

| **Minister:** | The years of our lives are a cup of wine poured out for us to drink. The grapes when they are pressed give forth their good juice for the wine. Under the wine press of time, our lives give forth their labor and honor and love. Many days will you sit at the same table and eat and drink together. Drink now, and may the cup of your lives be sweet and full to running over. |
| | [Bride and groom drink.] |

Rabbi:	Wine is a symbol of joy, of the richness of life and the sweetness of love. It is appropriate, therefore, that on this happy occasion, you toast life with this ancient symbol.
	This particular wine is especially significant: [Bride]'s maternal grandfather created this wine in his cellar more than 13 years ago; it has been nurtured and seasoned since then by [Bride]'s parents in anticipation of today's celebration.
	[See page 70, no. 3, for a transliteration of the Hebrew. Rabbi hands wine to bride, who drinks and passes it to groom.]

SEVEN HEBREW WEDDING BLESSINGS

Explanation of the Seven Wedding Blessings

The First Blessing is "Kiddush"—sanctification of God's name over the wine.

The Second and Third Blessings celebrate the theme of creation in a sequence that builds to the blessing of marriage.

The Fourth Blessing is a challenge to fulfill the potential for creativity, blessing, and peace.

The Fifth Blessing affirms that the bride and groom's marriage is made up of both passion and friendship.

The Sixth Blessing blesses the bride and groom separately. Their relationship as beloved companions requires that each be able to stand alone even as they come together, bringing individual gifts to the marriage.

The Seventh Blessing brings the bride and groom to rejoice together, united in gladness, surrounded by ten shades of joy and a chorus of jubilant voices.

A Literal Translation from the Hebrew

Blessed art Thou, O Lord our God, King of the universe, who created the fruit of the vine, symbol of joy.

Blessed art Thou, O Lord our God, King of the universe, who has created all things to Thy glory.

Blessed art Thou, O Lord our God, King of the universe, Creator of man.

Blessed art Thou, O Lord our God, King of the universe, who has made man in Thine image after Thy likeness, and has fashioned woman from man as his mate, that together they may perpetuate life. Blessed art Thou, O Lord, Creator of man.

May Zion rejoice as her children are restored to her in joy. Blessed art Thou, O Lord, who causes Zion to rejoice at her children's return.

O make these loved companions greatly to rejoice, even as of old Thou didst gladden Thy creatures in the Garden of Eden. Blessed art Thou, O Lord, who makest bridegroom and bride to rejoice.

Blessed art Thou, O Lord our God, King of the universe, who has created joy and gladness, bridegroom and bride, mirth and exultation, pleasure and delight, love, brother-hood, peace and fellowship. Soon may there be heard in the cities of Judah, and in the streets of Jerusalem, the voice of joy and gladness, the voice of the bridegroom and the voice of the bride, the jubilant voices of those joined in marriage under the bridal canopy, and of youths feasting and singing. Blessed art Thou, O Lord, who makest the bridegroom to rejoice with the bride.

Amen.

> **The only Jewish custom with which I was familiar at the time of our wedding was the sharing of the wine. Since we used a wine glass which had belonged to my great-great grandmother, we of course chose not to break it!**
>
> **— partner in an interfaith marriage**

An Alternative Translation

We acknowledge the Unity of all within the sovereignty of God, expressing our appreciation for this wine, symbol and aid of our rejoicing.

We acknowledge the Unity of all and realize that each separate moment and every distinct object points to and shares in the oneness.

We acknowledge the Unity of all within the sovereignty of God, recognizing and appreciating the blessing of being human.

May rejoicing resound throughout the world as the homeless are given homes, persecution and oppression cease, and all people learn to live in peace with each other and in harmony with the environment.

From the Divine source of all energy, we call forth an abundance of love to envelop this couple. May they be for each other lovers and friends, and may their love partake of the same innocence, purity and sense of discovery that we imagine the first couple to have experienced.

We acknowledge the Unity of all within the sovereignty of God, and we highlight today joy and gladness, bridegroom and bride, delight and cheer, love and harmony, peace and companionship. May we all witness the day when the dominant sounds throughout the world will be these sounds of happiness, the voices of lovers, the sounds of feasting and singing.

Praised to love, blessed be this marriage. May the bride and the bridegroom rejoice together.

An Adaptation To Be Recited by Congregation or Individual Friends and Family

We, your family and friends, wish for you the special joy of being a couple, making decisions together, sharing ideas, hopes and dreams, celebrating life's joys and confronting life's difficulties hand in hand.

We, your family and friends, bless you with our promise of continuing friendship and love to support you, encourage you, and enrich your lives.

Larry and Joanne exude happiness on their wedding day.

We, your family and friends, wish for you the strength to celebrate your uniqueness, honor your individuality, and complement each other in your differences.

We, your family and friends, bless you with days and nights filled with music, art, theater, books and the things that are special to each of you.

We, your family and friends, wish for you the wisdom to remember the community around you, to share the richness of your lives with others, to work toward justice and to contribute to the creation of a better world.

We, your family and friends, wish for you the freedom to explore, to imagine, to create. And we wish for you endless discovery of the world's treasures as well as the vision to appreciate the treasures of your selves.

We, your family and friends, bless you with a life filled with pleasure and warmth, humor and beauty, peace, friendship and love for each other!

— Rabbi Allen Secher

BENEDICTIONS

Officiant: [Bride] and [Groom]: As a collection of words, this ceremony would count for little, were it not for the love and commitment which you here pledge to one another. By virtue of being human, there is distance between you, which is both infinite and infinitesimal. Today you have joined in a convenant bridging that distance. Always remember that in reaching across any distance, you are faced with two choices: to circle the globe in one direction or to take one step in the other. May you ever seek the shorter distance, for love is as difficult—and as simple—as that.

Officiant: [Bride] and [Groom], you have now affirmed before your families and friends your love and your caring for each other. You have come from different backgrounds. You have walked different paths. You are different individuals. Your love has transcended these differences. In the years before you may the richness of the traditions that have nurtured you enhance and brighten your lives as you help to create and shape the future.

May the spirit of love be ever a part of your lives so that the union we here celebrate this day be worthy of continued celebration tomorrow and tomorrow and tomorrow.

....

Pastor and Rabbi: [See page 70, no. 2, for a transliteration of the Hebrew.]

May the God you worship be a blessing and a support to your lives.

May the God you honor help make your lives gracious and good.

May the God you serve be a light in your lives and bring you peace.

— from Unitarian readings

BREAKING OF THE GLASS

Officiant: Just as church bells are rung at the end of a Christian marriage, people of the Jewish faith smash a wine glass. Among the many interpretations of these two customs, one is that the loud noise of both church bells and breaking of the glass scares away evil spirits wishing harm to the newly married couple.

Breaking a glass summons the Jewish culture's notion that sweetness can only exist alongside bitterness—breaking the glass reminds us that although this wedding has provided joy, the world is still in turmoil, and requires our care and love. Its breaking is not only a reminder of sorrow, but also an expression of hope for a future free from all violence.

Frailty of the glass also suggests the frailty of human relationships. The glass, then, is broken to "protect" the marriage with an implied prayer, "As this glass shatters, so may your marriage never break."

....

Rabbi: In Jewish tradition the breaking of the glass at a wedding is a symbolic prayer and hope that your love for one another will remain until the pieces of this glass come together again. It is also a reminder that in the midst of all our rejoicing we should be mindful of all the want, pain and suffering that exist elsewhere in the world.

Since this is an interfaith ceremony, let us, with this symbol, be particularly mindful of the needless barriers that people erect between one another, and try to think, with the breaking of the glass, of breaking down those barriers and helping to build a world of respect, unity and peace.

[Rabbi puts glass under Bride and Groom's feet. Bride and Groom break the glass.
Bride and Groom kiss.]

HEBREW TRANSLITERATIONS

1. A Welcome

B'roochim Habaim B'shem Adonai

May you who come in the name of God be forever blessed.

2. A Benediction

Y'varechichah Adonai V'yishmirechah

May God bless and keep you.

Yaeyr Adonai Panav Eylechah Vichunehkah

May God cause the light of His countenance to shine upon you and be gracious unto you.

Yisah Adonai Panav Eylechah ViYasem L'chah Shalom

May God's presence be with you and grant you peace.

3. Kiddush

Baruch Atah Adonai Eloheynu Melech Ha-olam Borey P'ri Hagefen

We praise You, Adonai our God, ruler of the Universe, who has created the fruit of the vine.

4. A Prayer of Blessing

Mi Adir Al Hakol

Mi Gadol Al Hakol

Mi Baruch Al Hakol

Hu YiVarech et Hahatan V'et Hakallah

Most awesome, glorious and blessed God, guide and bless this bride and groom.

5. Wedding Blessing

Baruch Atah Adonai, M'kadesh Amo Al Y'dey Hupah V'Kidushin

We praise You, who hallows humankind through this sacred rite at the huppah.

The following three selections are all useful in conjunction with the exchange of rings.

6. Ring Ceremony

Harey At M'kudeshet Li B'taba-at Zu K'dat Eloheem U'bney Ahdam (said by male to female)

Harey Atah M'kudash Li B'taba-at Zu K'dat Eloheem U'bney Ahdam (said by female to male)

This ring is a symbol of your sacredness (or your specialness) unto me according to the ways of God and humanity.

(The above is a rephrasing of the traditional Jewish ring ceremony, which uses the phrase, "according to the laws of Moses and Israel," a phrase which in a mixed marriage might be considered inappropriate.)

7. Alternate Ring Ceremony

Dodi Li V'Ani Lah (male to female)

Dodi Li V'Ani Lo (female to male)

I am my beloved's and my beloved is mine.

(From the Biblical love poetry in Song of Songs)

8. Alternate Ring Ceremony

Zeh Dodi, Zeh Rey-i (same for male and female)

This is my beloved, this is my friend.

(Also from Song of Songs)

Please note:

1. These transliterations, graciously provided by Rabbi Allen Secher of Chicago, Illinois, are arbitrary and follow the modern Sefardit Hebrew used in most synagogues and in Israel.

   Also, there is absolutely no definitive translation. What Rabbi Secher tried to create is a translation that makes the most sense in the context of a wedding ceremony.

2. If you choose to include spoken Hebrew in your wedding ceremony, you might consider asking the Christian officiant to speak some of it. In this way, the ceremony will be seamless, and the speaking of Hebrew will not be considered an exclusively Jewish thing. Everyone wins when this happens—the Hebrew is demystified when Christian guests hear a priest or minister speaking it. The Jewish guests are reminded that they don't have a lock on the language or the ritual.

MUSICAL SELECTIONS

The following selections have been used in actual interfaith wedding ceremonies. One word of advice: in deference to the sensitivities of the Jewish family, you may want to avoid musical selections by known anti-semitic composers, such as Wagner's Wedding March.

Prelude

Anderson	"I'll Walk Beside You"
Bach	Brandenburg Concerto No. 3
	Concerto for Two Violins
	"Jesu, Joy of Man's Desiring"
Beethoven	"Ode to Joy"
Brahms	Hungarian Dance #4
Cooney/Daigle	"Covenant Hymn"
Copland	Shaker melody from "Appalachian Spring"
Hadar	"Erev Shel Shoshanim"
Israeli folk song	"Dodi Li"
John, Elton	"Love Song"

Mozart	"Eine Kleine Nachtmusik"	
Smetana, Bedrich	"The Moldau" from Ma Vlast	
Stookey, Paul	"The Wedding Song: There Is Love"	
Webber, Andrew Lloyd and Charles Hart	"All I Ask of You"	

Processional

Bach	Largo (from Xerxes)
Faure	Pavanne
Mouret	Masterpiece March
Pachelbel	Canon in D Major
Purcell	Trumpet Tune in C
	Trumpet Voluntary in D Major

Interlude

Bach	"Sheep May Safely Graze"
Bernstein	"One Hand, One Heart" (played while lighting Unity candle)
Bock, Jerry, and S. Harnick	"Sunrise, Sunset"
	"Sabbath Prayer"
Gordon, Peggy	"By My Side"
Raye, Collin	"In This Life"
Schubert	"Ave Maria"
Webber, Andrew Lloyd	"Love Changes Everything"
Wren, Brian	"When Love is Found"

Recessional

Clarke, Jeremiah	Trumpet Voluntary in D Major
Handel	Allegro; Water Music Suite
	Hornpipe; Water Music Suite
	"Bourree"
	"La Rejoussance"
Mendelssohn	"Wedding March" from Midsummer Night's Dream
Mouret	"Air Rondeau"
Strauss	"Die Fledermaus"
Vivaldi	Spring Allegro; The Four Seasons

[Note: Many of these selections appeared in different parts of different ceremonies.]

CHAPTER SIX

CREATING A WEDDING PROGRAM

nce you've gotten your ceremony written, you may want to produce a wedding program to share with guests on your wedding day. Such a program is particularly helpful in conjunction with interfaith wedding ceremonies, because chances are good that many people attending your wedding will not be familiar with all of the rituals and traditions you've chosen to include in your ceremony.

Many interfaith couples choose to include on the back cover of their wedding program a list of symbols and rituals they have incorporated into their ceremony, along with a brief explanation of their significance. Following is an adaptation of such a list, developed by couples and clergy affiliated with the Jewish-Catholic Couples Dialogue Group in Chicago, Illinois.

AN EXPLANATION OF THE RITUALS

To our families and friends,

Thank you for sharing our happiness with us today. Because some of the symbols and traditions of our ceremony may be unfamiliar, we have included some brief explanations.

The Huppah is a wedding canopy signifying that the bride and groom are joining together under one roof.

The Handshake of Peace is a tradition that gives members of the congregation the chance to share a visual sign of fellowship. We hope you will turn to someone that you have not met, and introduce yourself. Or turn to someone you do know, and share the joy of this day.

The Presentation of Roses to parents is drawn from the Catholic tradition of honoring the Virgin Mary with flowers before a wedding ceremony to foster fertility. It is a way of recognizing publicly the importance of our roots in our respective families.

The Kiddush Cup of wine is symbolic of the cup of life. It is used when saying the prayer for the sanctification of wine on the Sabbath and on holidays. As we share one cup of wine, we undertake the sharing of all that the future may bring. In Jewish tradition, the sweetness of the wine represents the joy of the occasion.

The Prayers of the Faithful are special petitions offered to God during a particular service or Mass. We have asked the members of our wedding party to compose their own prayers. Please feel free to add your own prayers, too.

The Ketubah is the Jewish legal marriage document with a legacy spanning two thousand years. In days past it served as protection for the bride should she lose her husband.

The Unity Candle is a visual expression of the unity of people with each other, and with God. With flames taken from the candles lit by our parents, we will be lighting a Havdalah Candle which is made of two wicks, intertwined, to symbolize that even in unity, we can remain individuals. A havdalah candle is traditionally lit at the end of the Sabbath.

A **Yarmulke**, **Kipa**, or skull cap, is worn by many Jews while praying. Some choose to wear one all the time. Wearing one reminds us that God is always above us.

The Breaking of the Glass is a tradition with several meanings. It teaches us that in times of joy we must also realize life brings sadness and sorrow. The sound of the breaking glass is said to frighten away evil spirits who might spoil this joyous occasion with their mischief. It also warns us that love, like glass, is fragile and must be protected. The promises made by the bride and groom, like the broken glass, are irrevocable. The breaking of the glass also reminds us of the destruction of the Second Temple in Jerusalem in 70 A.D.

Mazel Tov means good luck! And we wish that for all of you, with our love.

QUOTATIONS

Your wedding program can also be a good place to include all the beautiful passages and quotes that just won't fit into the actual ceremony itself. One couple constructed an eight-page program, complete with the texts of the readings and songs included in their ceremony and the translations of the Hebrew blessings. At the bottom of each page, separate from the body of the ceremony text, they placed one or two quotes that had meaning to them. Their choices ranged from Mark Twain to Dante to the New Testament. In this way they were able to include short passages that otherwise would have been left out of their wedding, and they gave guests something to browse while they awaited the start of the ceremony.

AN OPEN LETTER

A number of couples have used a portion of their wedding program to publicly thank their families, and to give a brief written glimpse into their thoughts as they become an interfaith couple. This "letter to the congregation" is often placed on the back cover of the program. Following are two examples of such an open letter to families and guests.

We would like to thank everyone for sharing this special day with us.

Our ceremony reflects both the Catholic and Jewish faiths and represents not only our union as two individuals, but the union of our families, our traditions, and our religions.

To our family and friends, we thank you for your love, laughter, and friendship.

We have wonderful memories of yesterday, and we look forward to all the memories yet to be made.

....

Dear Relatives and Friends,

It is with great joy that we welcome you to our wedding! We feel a miracle has happened here. Two unique people from different backgrounds and traditions grew up, studied and worked in different parts of the country. Finally, their paths crossed. They noticed one another. The seed of love was planted and grew. We are those people and we invite you to join us in thanking God for bringing us together.

There are a number of ways to create a beautiful and meaningful wedding program that will help your guests through your interfaith ceremony.

If we could summarize the thoughts and feelings we're trying to express in our ceremony today, they would probably fall into three themes:

1) We want to publicly pledge and celebrate our love for each other.

2) We want to take time to reflect on God, the author and prime example of love, commitment, fidelity, and growth.

3) We want to thank you for shaping our lives with your love and friendship and ask your continued support.

> **While falling in love is effortless and requires no work or output of energy, growing in love is work. It takes continual effort, and demands an on-going output of concentrated energy.**
>
> — **Christopher C. Reilly,**
>   *Making Your Marriage Work*

We feel that this is a very sacred moment in our lives. Even though we come from different faith traditions, we share a belief in a common God and religious values. We feel that God brought us together and has sustained us through our relationship. In fact, we feel that we are blessed to have two traditions, and hope to pass on to our children the best of both Judaism and Christianity. For this reason, the songs, prayers, actions, and readings in this ceremony were picked with great care. They reflect our greatest hopes for this moment and our future life together. Whatever your religious orientation, let us join together in praying for God's blessing on our marriage.

Part of what has made our wedding preparation special to us is our attempt to call on the talents of our friends as we plan the details of our ceremony. So that you are not strangers to one another, please allow us to introduce some of the people who have a special part in today's festivities.

The Families

[List the members of each partner's family.]

The Wedding Party

[Include a paragraph about the maid of honor and the best man.]

Ceremony Participants

[List the officiants, the ushers, the greeters, and the musicians.]

You

Last, but not least, we'd like to thank YOU for being here. Your presence and support are very important to us. Your generosity and best wishes have been truly moving. We will keep you forever in our hearts.

Afterword

It's hard to imagine, but before long, you'll have finished planning and organizing, and your big day will arrive. You'll have a fantastic wedding, the ceremony will be full of meaning and love, and your guests will compliment you on such a sensitive and inspiring ritual. After you get back from the honeymoon, send us a copy of your wedding ceremony, with your comments and reflections. We'll consider it for inclusion in the next edition of this book.

Send your ceremony, program, and reflections on your wedding day to:
Dovetail Publishing
P.O. Box 19945
Kalamazoo, MI 49019
fax: (616) 342-1012
e-mail: dovetail@mich.com

And when your wedding day is over, we hope that the beautiful memories of what you created will serve as a foundation for your successful intermarriage. As you begin the lifelong adventure of growing in love, remember to rely on the resources you've consulted—other interfaith families, supportive clergypeople, and books and periodicals designed to help you work through the issues you'll face (from celebrating holidays to raising children to communicating with your two families). Remember always that honest, open communication between you and your partner will be the bedrock of your long and successful interfaith marriage.

If yours will be an interreligious marriage, you presumably have already passed through [an] agonizing period and arrived at a livable solution. Have no fear. No life and no marriage are perfect. There are always differences to be accepted. Religious ones generally touch us more deeply and require a greater willingness to understand. But we can adjust to them, too, and even grow greatly in the process.

The real issue, however, centers not on the husband and wife but around the children who will come from this union. Two adults in love very likely could come to accept and respect each other's religious sentiments. Deciding on which faith to raise daughters and sons in is not settled so easily. That decision, nevertheless, should be reached whenever possible *before* a couple marries. To postpone this admittedly hard judgment until after the wedding will almost certainly create severe crises a few years later in marriage.

— Father Joseph M. Champlin,
Together for Life

RECOMMENDED RESOURCES

Please note: The following resources have been chosen from a wide variety of available books on weddings and wedding planning, and are recommended here based on their open-mindedness, practicality, and/or solid advice for interfaith couples. Resources marked with an asterisk (*) are highly recommended and should be added to every interfaith couple's library.

BOOKS ON PLANNING YOUR WEDDING CEREMONY:

Religious Help

Batts, Sidney F. *The Protestant Wedding Sourcebook: A Complete Guide for Developing Your Own Service*. Louisville, KY: Westminster/John Knox Press, 1993.

> Includes the texts of sample wedding services from 11 Protestant denominations.

Brill, Mordecai L., Marlene Halpin, and William H. Genné, eds. *Write Your Own Wedding*. Clinton, NJ: New Win Publishing, Inc., 1985.

> Edited by a Jew, a Catholic, and a Protestant. Contains samples of a contemporary and a traditional ceremony from each of these three traditions. Also contains an extensive list of appropriate musical selections.

Champlin, Joseph M. *Together For Life*. Notre Dame, IN: Ave Maria Press, 1970, 1988.

> A widely distributed Roman Catholic workbook for engaged couples. The appendix contains a very useful section on Catholic/non-Catholic intermarriage.

Diamant, Anita. *The New Jewish Wedding*. New York: Summit Books, 1985.

> The appendix contains an interfaith wedding ceremony entitled "Children of Noah," which reflects "the motif of the Rainbow Covenant, that not only the whole human race but all forms of life are in covenant with God."

Magida, Arthur J. *How to Be a Perfect Stranger: A Guide to Etiquette in Other People's Religious Ceremonies*. Woodstock, Vermont: Jewish Lights Publishing, 1996.

General Help

Glusker, David, and Peter Misner. *Words for Your Wedding: The Wedding Service Book*. HarperSanFrancisco, 1983, 1986.

Kingma, Daphne Rose. *Weddings from the Heart: Contemporary and Traditional Ceremonies for an Unforgettable Wedding*. Berkeley, CA: Conari Press, 1991, 1995.

Klausner, Abraham J. *Weddings: A Complete Guide to All Religious and Interfaith Marriage Services.* Columbus, OH: Alpha Publishing Company, 1986.

> Includes a chapter on interfaith weddings, as well as some very basic sample interfaith wedding ceremonies.

Metrick, Sydney Barbara. *I Do: A Guide to Creating Your Own Unique Wedding Ceremony.* Berkeley, CA: Celestial Arts, 1992.

Munro, Eleanor. *Wedding Readings: Centuries of Writing and Rituals for Love and Marriage.* New York: Viking, 1989.

Rogers, Jennifer. *Tried and Trousseau: The Bride Guide.* New York: Fireside (Simon & Schuster), 1992.

Stoner, Carroll. *Weddings for Grownups.* San Francisco: Chronicle Books, 1993.

Writing Your Vows

Eklof, Barbara. *With These Words. . . I Thee Wed: Contemporary Wedding Vows For Today's Couples.* Holbrook, MA: Adams Publishing, 1989.

Kehret, Peg. *Wedding Vows: How to express your love in your own words.* Colorado Springs, CO: Meriwether Publishing Ltd., 1989.

BOOKS ON INTERFAITH MARRIAGE

*Crohn, Joel, Ph.D. *Mixed Matches: How to Create Successful Interracial, Interethnic, and Interfaith Marriages.* New York: Fawcett Columbine, 1995.

Gruzen, Lee. *Raising Your Jewish/Christian Child: How Interfaith Parents Can Give Children the Best of Both Their Heritages.* New York: Newmarket Press, 1990.

Mayer, Egon. *Love and Tradition: Marriage Between Jews and Christians.* New York: Plenum, 1985.

*Petsonk, Judy, and Jim Remsen. *The Intermarriage Handbook.* New York: William Morrow, 1988.

> Contains a sample wedding ceremony described as "a universalist ceremony with Jewish content." Also contains an excellent overview of the history of Jewish/Christian relations (chapter one) and a useful chapter called "Should You Get Married?" (chapter two).

Reuben, Steven Carr, Ph.D. *Making Interfaith Marriage Work.* Rocklin, CA: Prima Publishing, 1994.

> Can be ordered directly from the publisher by calling (916) 632-4400.

*Rosenbaum, Mary Heléne and Stanley Ned. *Celebrating Our Differences: Living Two Faiths in One Marriage*. Boston, Kentucky: Ragged Edge Press and Black Bear Productions, 1994.

> Can be ordered directly from the publisher by sending $19.95 plus $3.50 shipping and handling to: Black Bear Productions, P.O. Box 1110, Carlisle, PA 17013-6110.

Rosenberg, Rabbi Roy A., Father Peter Meehan, and Rev. John Wade Payne. *Happily Intermarried: Authoritative Advice for a Joyous Jewish-Christian Marriage*. New York: Collier Books, Macmillan Publishing Company, 1988.

> This book is out of print but worth looking for in your local library or used bookstore.

Schneider, Susan Weidman. *Intermarriage: The Challenge of Living with Differences Between Christians & Jews*. New York: The Free Press, 1989.

BOOKS ON MARRIAGE IN GENERAL

Dahl, Stephanie. *Modern Bride® Just Married*. New York: John Wiley & Sons, 1994.

Greteman, James. *Creating a Marriage*. Mahwah, NJ: Paulist Press, 1993.

Reilly, Christopher C. *Making Your Marriage Work: Growing in Love After Falling in Love*. Mystic, CT: Twenty-Third Publications, 1989.

BOOKS OF PRAYERS AND READINGS

Jegen, Sister Carol Frances, and Rabbi Byron L. Sherwin. *Thank God: Prayers of Jews and Christians Together*. Chicago: Liturgical Training Publications, 1989.

> You can order this book directly from the publisher by calling (800) 933-1800.

BOOKLETS/PAMPHLETS

"Interfaith Marriage: A Resource by Presbyterian Christians." Available for $1.50 from Distribution Management Services, 100 Witherspoon Street, Louisville, KY 40202-1396.

> You can order this booklet directly from the publisher by calling (800) 524-2612.

PERIODICALS

Dovetail: A Newsletter by and for Jewish/Christian Families
P.O. Box 19945, Kalamazoo, MI 49019

> This independent national publication can help engaged and newly married couples begin to address the various issues that will confront them in their life together as an interfaith family. A one-year subscription (six issues) is available for $24.99. You can order this periodical directly from the publisher by calling (800) 222-0070.

Rabbinic Center for Research and Counseling

128 East Dudley Avenue

Westfield, NJ 07090

(908) 233-2288

Rabbi Irwin H. Fishbein maintains a regularly updated list of Reform and Reconstructionist rabbis who officiate at interfaith wedding ceremonies. His list is available for a fee of $20.00. The list contains the names and telephone numbers of several hundred rabbis from coast to coast, along with each rabbi's stance on a number of different conditions and requirements under which they will perform a ceremony, from requesting conversion of the non-Jewish spouse to requiring that future children be raised as Jews. Please note that some rabbis who will officiate at interfaith weddings choose not to be included in this list, so it is worth inquiring locally in addition to reviewing this list. The Rabbinic Center also offers a workshop for interfaith couples on raising children in an intermarried home.

Ethical Culture

Leaders of this movement are often willing to officiate at interfaith ceremonies. Leaders (the equivalent of a minister or rabbi) are located in the greater metro New York area, Boston, Washington/Baltimore, Chicago, St. Louis, Texas, and Iowa. To arrange for an Ethical Cultural officiant for your ceremony, call (212) 873-6500.

Unitarian Universalist Association

Contact Nancy Hezlitt at (617) 742-2100, extension 408, for help with finding a local Unitarian Universalist clergyperson.

Noah Saunders

Noah is an ordained lay minister in Boulder, Colorado. He has amassed a great number of resources on and experiences with interfaith wedding ceremonies, and he is happy to be contacted at:

Noah R. W. Saunders

3990 Pleasant Ridge Rd.

Boulder, CO 80301

e-mail: 73061.31@compuserve.com

Interfaith Ketubot (Wedding Covenants)

Good Company

P.O. Box 3218

Chicago, IL 60654

(312) 913-9193

Produces a six-color interfaith ketubah with language that expresses a couple's commitment to respect each other's heritage.

Caspi Cards & Art

P.O. Box 220

Newtonville, MA 02160

(617) 964-8888

Produces several ketubah designs with language for partners of different heritages.

Interfaith Support Groups

The following list of support groups for interfaith families is excerpted from the Bulletin Board section of *Dovetail: A Newsletter by and for Jewish/Christian Families*, and was current as we went to press with this book in March 1996.

Amherst, Massachusetts

Two existing local interfaith groups.

Contact: Janet Lehan Bloom

(413) 253-3685

New Haven, Connecticut

Existing interfaith group.

Contact: Christina Giebisch-Mohrer

(203) 287-9110

Rockland County, New York

Interested in forming an interfaith group.

Contact: Eric and Elizabeth Kohlmeier

(914) 639-9380

Capital District Area, New York

Interested in either joining an existing group or forming a new group.

Contact: John and Debbie Toy

(518) 439-3451

South Jersey/Philadelphia

Bifaithful Families & Children Network

Contact: Miriam Gilbert, (609) 753-1173

Greater Washington, DC, Area

Interfaith Families Project

Existing interfaith group.

Contact: Laura Steinberg

(301) 589-9280

Atlanta, Georgia

Interested in starting a support group.

Contact: Mitch Wynn and Yvonne Evans

(404) 495-1474

Memphis, Tennessee

Newly-formed interfaith group.

Contact: Jan and David Kaplan

(901) 767-4267

Louisville, Kentucky

Interested in forming an interfaith group.

Contact: Carolyn Humphrey & Fred Gross

(502) 423-8583

Cincinnati, Ohio

Interested in joining an interfaith group.

Contact: Christine M. Segal

(513) 489-8840, ext. 276 (day)

(513) 793-2866 (evening)

Minneapolis, Minnesota

Twin Cities Support Group

Existing interfaith group.

Contact: Chris Simon & Judy Sharken Simon

(612) 724-8947

Chicago, Illinois

Jewish-Catholic Couples Dialogue Group

Existing interfaith group.

Contact: Patty and David Kovacs

(312) 275-5689, or

Abbe and Dan Josephs, (708) 963-4565

Tulsa, Oklahoma

Newly-formed group for families interested
in celebrating both religions.

Contact: Sally Nahmias

(918) 298-5959

Denver, Colorado

Interested in forming an interfaith group.

Contact: Karen McCarthy and Dan Kowal

(303) 439-7750

San Francisco Bay Area, California

Existing interfaith group.

Contact: Alicia Torre

(415) 591-9434

PERMISSIONS

We gratefully acknowledge permission from the following couples
and clergy to reprint from their wedding ceremonies.

Nancy and Harry Cohen

Kathryn and Lance Flitter

Renita Gordon and Michael Miller

Patty and David Kovacs

Karen McCarthy and Dan Kowal

Rabbi Steve Mason

Pam and Larry Rosenberg

Father Albert Ruschman

Noah Saunders

Rabbi Allen Secher

Helen and Tom Shibley

Susannah West and David Powell

ABOUT THE AUTHOR

Joan C. Hawxhurst is the editor of *Dovetail: A Newsletter By and For Jewish/Christian Families*, an independent national periodical devoted to the challenges and opportunities facing inter-faith families. A practicing United Methodist, Joan lives with her Jewish husband and daughter in Kalamazoo, Michigan. She founded *Dovetail* in 1992 upon realizing that interfaith families had a difficult time finding resources that balance and respect the faiths of both partners. She believed that interfaith families needed an independent vehicle to share experiences and support each other. With an MA in international relations from Yale University and ten years of writing and editing experience, Joan decided to create a new kind of resource, and *Dovetail* was born.

Prior to starting *Dovetail*, Joan worked for the Board of Global Ministries of the United Methodist Church, spending time in Argentina and Washington, DC, working with human rights organizations. She currently serves on the Interfaith Relations Commission of the National Council of Churches. She is the author of several books for grade school students as well as numerous articles for national periodicals, on topics ranging from interfaith marriage to international debt in South America. She has been married for five years to Steven B. Bertman and is the mother of two-year-old Sarah Jane Bertman.

THE PERFECT KEEPSAKE FOR INTERFAITH COUPLES

The Ketubah, or Hebrew marriage contract, has been a tradition since ancient times. The intent of this tradition is powerful and its meaning universal. A ceremonial and artistic document, a Ketubah witnesses a bride and groom's promise and commitment to love and honor one another.

Now, for the first time, a Ketubah is available in language especially suited to interfaith couples. Rabbi Allen Secher of Chicago adapted the text and collaborated with an artist and a specialist in typography and fine printing to create this unique piece. The poetic and egalitarian style clearly expresses an interfaith couple's commitment to respect each other's heritage. It is a beautiful art piece, a keepsake and an ideal gift to reflect your love and support.

To order by telephone:
312-913-9193
Express delivery available.

To order by mail, complete the form and send it to:

COMPANY

P.O. Box 3218
Chicago, IL 60654

Actual size: 16 x 20 inches in six vibrant colors

☐ Send me the free, full-color miniature reproduction. I want to examine the colors and text before ordering.

☐ Send me the full-size Ketubah. Enclosed is $95 plus $10 shipping and handling. (IL residents add $6 tax.)

Name

Address

City/State/Zip

Telephone

Mishpucha et al

Interfaith Greeting Cards in the Holiday Spirit

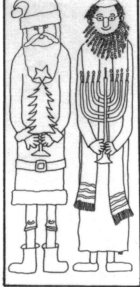

A unique selection of whimsical, warm-hearted, witty designs for the holidays...the perfect ecumenical solution for interfaith families to send or receive. Brightly colored drawings by Patricia Goodman, a partner herself in a successful interfaith marriage. Call or write for a free brochure!

And featuring...our charming interfaith wedding design. Perfect for use as an imaginative wedding invitation or for personal thank you notes. Matching response cards and lined envelopes are available.

a division of
PATNIE PAPERS 223 Katonah Avenue, Katonah, NY 10536
Ph: (914) 232-3653, Fx: (914) 232-3584, Toll-Free: (800) 764-0953

Bubbe & Gram: My Two Grandmothers

by Joan C. Hawxhurst
illustrated by Jane K. Bynum
hardcover, 32 pages, $12.95.

Winner of the 1997 Benjamin Franklin Silver Medal Award for excellence in independent publishing, in the parenting category.

A warm, supportive story for children in interfaith families, **Bubbe and Gram: My Two Grandmothers** relates the touching story of a child who loves and learns from her two very different grandmothers. Her Jewish Bubbe tells stories about Moses and the Maccabees, lights the Sabbath candles and shares Passover with her grandchild. Her Christian Gram dyes Easter eggs with her granddaughter, recites the Lord's Prayer and tells the Nativity story. Each grandmother shares the love and richness of her own tradition with her grandchild, while still respecting the other religious tradition that is part of the little girl's life.

Children will love being able to identify with the little girl as she explores the traditions and holidays of both Christianity and Judaism. Parents and grandparents will welcome the opportunity to share their diverse and valuable faith experiences with the children in their lives.

Another quality publication for interfaith families from
Dovetail Publishing, Inc., P.O. Box 19945, Kalamazoo, MI 49019, (616) 342-2900

" **Bynum's crinkle-eyed, ever-smiling characters emphasize the stress-free dynamics of the interfaith relationships here portrayed. Both religions are given equal time in this book that will be of particular interest to interfaith families."**
—*Publisher's Weekly*, 1/27/97

" [*Bubbe & Gram*] shows a child enriched by her bonds with her Jewish and Christian grandmothers. The loving message is clear: this child is lucky to have Christmas and Hanukkah, Passover and Easter, and stories from everywhere."
—*Booklist*, 1/1/97

Dovetail: A Journal by and for Jewish/Christian Families

Since 1992, **Dovetail** has brought balanced and non-judgmental coverage of issues of interest to interfaith families to its growing list of readers around the nation. *Library Journal* calls **Dovetail** a "valuable and sincerely open-minded channel of communication."

Dovetail is

- the first periodical to balance and respect the perspectives of both Jewish and Christian partners in interfaith marriages.

- an important source of information and resources for interfaith couples, their parents, and their children.

- a bimonthly channel of communication for interfaith families, designed to foster sharing of ideas, experiences, and support.

- a lively mixture of useful and exciting articles, interviews, columns by religious and lay experts, book reviews, excerpts, and resources lists.

- an independent and dynamic periodical that encourages reader involvement and responds to its readers' needs and wishes.

Dovetail
A Journal by and for Jewish/Christian Families

What Can We Learn from Other Kinds of Interfaith Families?

For more than four years now, Dovetail has been exploring the challenges and opportunities of life in this time, we have received countless requests for information from couples whose dual-faith families included religious traditions other than Christianity and Judaism. In this issue of Dovetail, we seek to examine life in other kinds of interfaith families, with two goals: to compare the challenges we in Jewish/Christian families face with those other interfaith families face, and to see how our common struggles put all of us in a unique and transformative position. We all share the challenges of respecting two distinct heritages within one marriage, of navigating uncomfortable boundary lines, of being true to our own nuclear families while maintaining connections with our extended families. We can learn from one another, and we can join forces to combat intolerance.

A *Time* magazine article on inter-married couples (Fall 1993 issue, pp. 64-65), which included profiles of Jewish/Christian, Hindu/Christian and Buddhist/Christian families, opined that "the world still has much to learn about living with diversity. [The pain of intolerance] is evidence that America has yet to harvest the full rewards of its founding principles. The land of immigrants may be giving way to a land of hyphenations, but the hyphen still divides even as it compounds. Those who intermarry have

perhaps the strongest sense of what it will take to return America to an unhyphenated whole."

In other parts of the world interfaith couples face much more difficult responses to their decision to marry. In the former Yugoslavia, dual-faith marriages are the source of much controversy. Before the war, 45 percent of the families living in Sarajevo were mixed. In response to the anguish caused by the war, the Islamic community and some segments of the press have called for mixed marriages to be banned. "Most mixed marriages break down," wrote a columnist in late 1994 in Sarajevo's daily *Ljiljan* (as

In This Issue

October/November 1996

Volume 5, Number 2

A one-year subscription (six issues) is $24.99; international subscriptions are $35.00.

Send in the coupon at the back of this book for a free sample issue.

Or call 800-222-0070 to start your subscription today.

You Can Purchase
Back Issues of **Dovetail**

The following back issues of **Dovetail** are currently available:

Issue 1:5: **Grandparents of Interfaith Children**

Issue 2:1: **Religious Education for Your Interfaith Children:
How to Decide**

Issue 2:4: **Welcoming Ceremonies: Bringing an Interfaith
Child into the Community**

Issue 2:5: **Intermarried Clergy: Special Jewish-Christian Harmony**

Issue 2:6: **Adult Children of Intermarriage Share Their Stories**

Issue 3:3: **Seeking Therapy: When Interfaith Couples Need Help**

Issue 3:4: **The Special Circumstances of Death in an Interfaith Family**

Issue 3:5: **Passover and Easter: Two Faiths' Celebrations of the Spring**

Issue 3:6: **Coming of Age in an Interfaith Family**

Issue 4:1: **Children and Change: Divorce and Adoption in Interfaith Families**

Issue 4:4: **Looking Back on our Interfaith Wedding Ceremonies: Insights and Advice**

Issue 4:5: **How Jewish Institutions are Responding to Intermarriage**

Issue 4:6: **Raising Children in Two Faiths: What Does It Really Mean?**

Issue 5:1: **How Can Interfaith Families Worship Together?**

Issue 5:2: **What Can We Learn from Other Interfaith Families?**

Issue 5:3: **Choosing A Single Faith for Your Household: Couples Who Make this Choice**

Issue 5:4: **Clergy Speak Out on Intermarriage at National Workshop**

Issue 5:5: **Laughter is the Best Medicine: Humor in an Interfaith Family**

Issue 5:6: **Research on Children and Religious Education in Interfaith Families**

Issue 6:1: **How to Start Your Own Interfaith Couples' Support Group**

Issue 6:2: **Enjoying Christmas and Hanukkah: Shining Through the Season of Stars**

Send $4.50 per issue to:
DOVETAIL Publishing
P.O. Box 19945
Kalamazoo, MI 49019

Quantities are limited, so order today!

New Title from Dovetail Publishing:

The Interfaith Family Guidebook: Practical Advice for Jewish and Christian Partners

by Joan C. Hawxhurst

0-9651284-4-X

192 pages, softcover, $16.95

Available March 1998

Over one million Jewish/Christian families in the United States face the challenges and opportunities inherent in their decision to marry. Many thousands of these families are struggling to define their households' faith choices and traditions without the help of religious institutions. The only comprehensive guide in print for families living with two faiths in one household, **The Interfaith Family Guidebook** offers these families a look at the many questions they will face and the resources available to help them find their own answers.

This concise and practical guidebook will help interfaith couples to:

- Respect and appreciate both of their religious heritages
- Discuss with candor the struggles they will face
- Celebrate all the holidays that are meaningful to them
- Nurture positive relationships with their extended families
- Create a mutually satisfactory plan for celebrating in their home
- Decide how to raise their children
- Plan meaningful ceremonies to mark their marriage, the birth of a child, coming-of-age, and other life-cycle events
- Learn from the experiences of other interfaith families
- Find helpful local and national resources and support groups

> **To order, call 800-222-0070 or send your check for $16.95 + $4.50 shipping/handling to Dovetail Publishing, P.O. Box 19945, Kalamazoo, MI 49019.**

This book is for interfaith families who are committed to understanding both religious traditions and to communicating about their unique perspectives as Christians and Jews who have chosen to marry. Full of nonjudgmental information and resources, this book is a valuable tool that will be turned to again and again by Jewish/Christian families, their parents and children, and the professionals who serve them.

The Interfaith Family Guidebook comes from the nationally acclaimed publisher of **Dovetail: A Journal by and for Jewish/Christian Families**, the pre-eminent independent source of information and resources for interfaith families. **Dovetail**, the first periodical to balance and respect the perspectives of both Christian and Jewish partners in interfaith marriages, has been published since 1992 by an experienced editorial team of academics, clergy, counselors and interfaith couples themselves.

Individually handmade and handglazed pottery. Perfectly suited to an interfaith ceremony.

A beautiful part of your interfaith wedding ceremony, and an heirloom that your family will treasure for many Shabbat dinners and life-cycle celebrations to come.

The three-piece set includes:

- Kiddish Cup with a Star of David symbol
- Chalice (identical to the Kiddish Cup) with a Cross symbol
- Challah Plate/Shabbat Tray with Dove symbol (can be used during the wedding ceremony to hold both cups)

The clay used is high-fired stoneware, very durable and dishwasher safe. The glaze—gemlike and luminous—is shades of robin's egg blue of overlapping thicknesses, against a contrasting bone white stem. Each item is individually done and invites careful attention.

The artist is Sara K. Rubin, herself a partner in a marriage of differing religious/cultural backgrounds. Ms. Rubin has her M.F.A. in Ceramics and Ceramic Sculpture from RIT in Rochester, NY. Because of her lifelong interest in spirituality, most of her pottery relates to contemporary religious themes.

The Kiddish Cup and Chalice are each 6-1/2" to 7" tall and hold approximately eight ounces of fluid.

The Challah Plate/Shabbat Tray is approximately 8" by 10-1/2", and can be used both as a tray for the two celebration cups and as a serving piece for challah during weekly Shabbat observances.

The cost of this exquisite and unique set is $151.99, which includes shipping and special protective packaging. Allow 3-4 weeks for delivery.

To order, call 888-R-FAITHS (888-732-4847) or send your check for $151.99 to Dovetail Publishing, P.O. Box 19945, Kalamazoo, MI 49019.

Helpful Resources for Interfaith Families

The following products are endorsed by Dovetail Publishing as valuable resources for interfaith families. All of the following products can be ordered with a VISA or MasterCard by calling **Dovetail at 888-R-FAITHS (888-732-4847)**. Or send your check or money order, for the product total plus shipping and handling ($4.50 for the first item, $1.00 additional for each additional product), to: Dovetail Catalog Group, PO Box 19945, Kalamazoo, MI 49019.

A Traveling Jewish Theatre's
An Open Gate: An Exploration of Jewish/Christian Intermarriage
Cassette tape, $12.50.

This audio cassette tape features excerpts from ATJT's play, *Heart of the World*, which explores the potency of one's cultural and religious past, and faces the dilemmas—from circumcision to Christmas—that arise when two people come from different traditions. This inclusive and non-judgmental recording, featuring interviews with clergy and members of Jewish/Christian families, focuses on the variety of ways interfaith families reconcile their differences and find community.

Raising Your Jewish/Christian Child: How Interfaith Parents Can Give Children the Best of Both Their Heritages
by Lee F. Gruzen
Softcover, 272 pp., $10.95.

Based on personal experience, extensive research, and hundreds of interviews with families, clergypeople, educators, sociologists, and psychologists, Lee Ferguson Gruzen, an award-winning TV producer, writer, and mother of her own interfaith family, provides sorely needed advice on how to incorporate both Jewish and Christian faiths into a family's lifestyle. Positively, supportively, this book—including forewords by a distinguished minister and rabbi—discusses the wide variety of choices made by interfaith families, making a strong case for giving children an understanding and respect for both heritages.

Between Two Worlds: Choices for Grown Children of Jewish-Christian Parents
by Leslie Goodman-Malamuth & Robin Margolis
Softcover, 208 pp., $10.00.

Parents in dual-faith families who face the difficult issue of religious education for their children will be heartened and helped by this book written by two grown children of interfaith marriage. Based on personal experiences and on hundreds of interviews with other adult children of intermarriage, **Between Two Worlds** is frank about the challenges—and opportunities— facing kids who grow up in a dual-faith home.

Mixed Matches: How to Create Successful Interracial, Interethnic, and Interfaith Relationships
by Joel Crohn, Ph.D.
Softcover, 335 pp., $12.00.

Psychotherapist Joel Crohn has learned in years of counseling couples in cross-cultural relationships that *how* partners negotiate their cultural and religious differences is as important as *what* the differences are. The methods in **Mixed Matches** have helped many couples approach each other compassionately, teaching them to "translate" their different styles of expression and negotiate successful resolutions. Dr. Crohn also offers practical advice on how couples can confront prejudice and stereotypes, deal with in-laws, and help children achieve a sense of identity.

Thank God: Prayers of Jews and Christians Together
by Carol Frances Jegen, BVM and Rabbi Byron L. Sherwin
Softcover, 58 pp., $6.50.

The texts in this collection are prayers and brief orders of service to be used at home, in small groups or in interfaith services. Wording is suitable for use by both Jews and Christians. Useful for planning wedding and other life-cycle ceremonies where both Jews and Christians will be present.

Resources to Help Interfaith Families Resolve the "December Dilemma"

The following Hanukkah and Christmas products are endorsed by Dovetail Publishing as valuable resources for interfaith families. All of the following products can be ordered with a VISA or MasterCard by calling Dovetail at 888-R-FAITHS (888-732-4847). Or send your check or money order, for the product total plus shipping and handling ($4.50 for the first item, $1.00 additional for each additional product), to: Dovetail Catalog Group, PO Box 19945, Kalamazoo, MI 49019.

Hanukkah and Christmas at My House

written and illustrated by Susan Enid Gertz
Softcover, 32 pp., navy and white illustrations, $6.95.
Share this quiet, thoughtful story about family love and holiday joys with the young child in your life. The book's message—for the interfaith child and all children—is that families of all religions love their children and their traditions, and the joy of the holidays that comes from that love. **Child** magazine calls it "a sensitive account of how to observe both holidays while preserving the integrity of each."

Candles, Snow and Mistletoe

by Sharon, Lois and Bram
CD $17.98, or audio cassette $11.98.

A delightful mix of Hanukkah songs, Christmas songs and winter celebration songs. "The popular Canadian vocal trio has assembled a holiday album crackling with freshly roasted chestnuts and some spunky new material. The group is careful to include songs that celebrate both Christmas and Hanukkah, as well as to give an international flavor to standards such as The Twelve Days of Christmas."
-*The Chicago Sun Times*

Christmas Crafts: Merry Things to Make, and
Hanukkah Fun: Crafts and Games

Softcovers, 32 pp. each, set of two, $8.90.

Colorful, large-format books are ideal for interfaith parents looking for fun ways to create their own holiday decorations and traditions with their children. Each book focuses on one winter holiday, with great ideas for holiday items made with simple materials and easy-to-follow directions. Make your own menorahs, holiday cards, ornaments, mobiles, gifts, and much more.

Handmade Reversible Hanukkah and Christmas Placemats

Set of four 12" by 18" placemats with coordinating napkins, $36.00.
12" by 54" table runner, $20.00.

With a Christmas motif on one side and Hanukkah symbols on the other, these table linens are the perfect solution for holiday meals and entertaining. Handmade by an at-home mom in Michigan, so order early!

NOTES

NOTES

ORDER FORM

Fax orders:	(616) 342-1012
Telephone orders:	Call Toll Free: (800) 222-0070
	Have your VISA or MasterCard information ready.
On-line orders:	Joan C. Hawxhurst, dovetail@mich.com
Postal orders:	Dovetail Publishing, P.O. Box 19945, Kalamazoo, MI 49019
	Telephone: (616) 342-2900

☐ Please send _____ copies of *Interfaith Wedding Ceremonies: Samples and Sources*
 ($19.95 per copy plus $4.50 one-time shipping and handling charge).

☐ Please send a one-year subscription to *Dovetail: A Journal by and for Jewish/Christian Families* ($24.99 for six bimonthly issues).

Name:

Address:

City:

State: Zip:

Telephone:

TOTAL Amount Due:

Sales tax: Please add 6% for books shipped to Michigan addresses.

Payment Method: ☐ check   Credit card: ☐ VISA   ☐ MasterCard

Card number: Exp. date:

Name on card:

Signature:

Call toll-free and order now.

ORDER FORM

Fax orders:	(616) 342-1012
Telephone orders:	Call Toll Free: (800) 222-0070
	Have your VISA or MasterCard information ready.
On-line orders:	Joan C. Hawxhurst, dovetail@mich.com
Postal orders:	Dovetail Publishing, P.O. Box 19945, Kalamazoo, MI 49019
	Telephone: (616) 342-2900

☐ Please send _____ copies of *Interfaith Wedding Ceremonies: Samples and Sources*
($19.95 per copy plus $4.50 one-time shipping and handling charge).

☐ Please send a one-year subscription to *Dovetail: A Journal by and for Jewish/Christian Families* ($24.99 for six bimonthly issues).

Name:

Address:

City:

State: Zip:

Telephone:

TOTAL Amount Due:

Sales tax: Please add 6% for books shipped to Michigan addresses.

Payment Method: ☐ check   Credit card: ☐ VISA   ☐ MasterCard

Card number: Exp. date:

Name on card:

Signature:

Call toll-free and order now.

Start out your married life on the right foot with help from a unique and supportive resource!

This coupon entitles the bearer to one complimentary sample issue of *Dovetail: A Journal by and for Jewish/Christian Families.*

Dovetail is an independent national periodical devoted to the challenges and opportunities of life in an interfaith family. We work hard to balance and respect the perspectives of both Jewish and Christian partners in interfaith marriages.

To redeem your coupon:

Fax it to: (616) 342-1012

Mail it to: Dovetail Publishing,
P. O. Box 19945,
Kalamazoo, MI 49019
(616) 342-2900

Dovetail should be mailed to:

Name: _____

Address: _____

City: _____

State: _____ Zip: _____

Telephone: _____

This coupon may not be reproduced and is for one-time use only.

Contact *Dovetail* today for your FREE sample issue.